COMPANIONS

So much more.

Companions in Christ® is *so much more* than printed resources. It is a community of people on a journey together. Our Companions Web site offers support for this journey through

- Opportunities to find other churches offering Companions in Christ groups for youth, children, and adults;

- Insights and testimonies from other Companions in Christ participants;

- Training opportunities that develop and deepen the leadership skills used in formational groups;

- Helpful leadership tips, articles, and downloadable resources;

- A regular e-newsletter offering spiritual formation insights and discounts on Companions resources;

- A promise to pray for your Companions group. (See "Prayers for Our *Way of Discernment* Group" page at the back of this book for information.)

Just complete this form and drop it in the mail to register yourself and your Companions group on the Companions Web site. OR, visit the Web site and enter your information there at www.CompanionsInChrist.org.

Name: _____

Address: _____

City/State/Zip: _____

Church: _____

E-mail: _____

Phone: _____

❏ Please register me to receive the Companions in Christ e-newsletter.
❏ Please keep me informed of spiritual formation events and resources from Upper Room Ministries.

Upper Room Ministries
P.O. Box 340012
Nashville, TN 37203-9540

COMPANIONS *in Christ*
A SMALL-GROUP EXPERIENCE IN SPIRITUAL FORMATION

The Way of DISCERNMENT

Leader's Guide

Marjorie J. Thompson

UPPER ROOM BOOKS®
NASHVILLE

For more information on *Companions in Christ,*
visit www.CompanionsInChrist.org or call 1-800-972-0433.

With deep gratitude and affection,

Upper Room Ministries dedicates this book

to the memory of Schuyler Bissell—

man of profound faith and integrity;

member of St. George's Episcopal Church, Nashville;

advisory group member, trainer, leader,

and unflagging advocate for Companions in Christ.

Contents

.

Acknowledgments

The original twenty-eight week *Companions in Christ* resource grew from the seeds of a vision long held by Stephen D. Bryant, world editor and publisher of Upper Room Ministries. It was given shape by Marjorie J. Thompson, director of Pathways in Congregational Spirituality with Upper Room Ministries and spiritual director for Companions in Christ. The vision, which has now expanded into the Companions in Christ series, was realized through the efforts of many people over many years. The original advisers, consultants, authors, editors, and test churches are acknowledged in the foundational twenty-eight-week resource. We continue to owe an immense debt of gratitude to each person and congregation named there.

Stephen V. Doughty wrote the weekly articles in *The Way of Discernment*. The daily exercises in the Participant's Book are principally the work of Marjorie Thompson. Marjorie wrote the Leader's Guide, developing some portions based on preliminary suggestions from Stephen Doughty. The Participant's Book and Leader's Guide benefited from input by a staff editorial team, including Stephen Bryant, Lynne Deming, Jerry Haas, and Susan Ruach.

Our profound thanks go to seven leaders in four statewide test groups, whose valuable feedback helped reshape elements of both the Participant's Book and Leader's Guide. These group leaders and the churches they represent included: Carmen Gaud and Diana Hynson, Edgehill United Methodist Church, Nashville, Tennessee; Amy Hutchinson-Cox and Linda Morley, Second Presbyterian Church, Nashville, Tennessee; Mary Jayne Allen, First Baptist Church, Chattanooga, Tennessee; and Rosita Echols and Jo Ann Powell, Westminster Presbyterian Church, Knoxville, Tennessee.

Introduction

Welcome to *Companions in Christ: The Way of Discernment,* a small-group resource designed to introduce the importance of spiritual discernment and to help participants experience a variety of personal and corporate discernment practices. Many such practices are being reclaimed from our Christian heritage and adapted to our current context. Indeed, discernment has become a topic of considerable interest to the church over the past decade, yet most congregations do not practice discernment, partly because it remains unfamiliar to most individual believers. This resource aims to help Christians learn the basics of discernment at a personal level, then move toward group practices that can begin to reshape church life at congregational and larger ecclesial levels. We hope that *The Way of Discernment* will reach many church leaders, both ordained and lay, who will find in it a helpful way to seed discernment practices in the body of Christ. However, it is designed to be accessible to anyone with sincere interest in listening deeply to the guidance of the Holy Spirit.

The Way of Discernment is the eighth title in the Companions in Christ series, a sequence of resources developed to help small groups deepen and expand the core spiritual practices introduced in the foundational twenty-eight-week *Companions in Christ* resource. Other resources in the Companions series (in addition to the foundational resource) include *The Way of Grace, The Way of Blessedness, The Way of Forgiveness, The Way of Transforming Discipleship,* and *The Way of Prayer.* An additional title, *Exploring the Way,* offers a basic introduction to spiritual formation in a format suitable to either a class or small group.

The Way of Discernment offers a ten-week journey (plus preparatory meeting) in exploring the principles and practices of personal spiritual discernment, along with several forms of small-group discernment. It points beyond the limitations of its own small-group structure to possibilities for the decision-making bodies of congregations and denominations. An appendix section includes helpful information on discernment and various approaches to this practice.

The movement from personal to corporate practice is, at one level, natural and organic. It is also intentional, based on the premise that the effectiveness of group discernment depends largely on the quality of its members' personal discernment. We trust that those who complete these ten weeks will come away with a clearer grasp of effective means for personal discernment, and both a greater desire and capacity to transfer the practices they have learned to larger church settings.

The Way of Discernment builds on Part 5 of the original twenty-eight-week *Companions* resource. That final segment, "Exploring Spiritual Guidance: The Spirit of Christ," addresses our understanding of God's will, spiritual guidance in pairs and groups, corporate discernment practices, and needs for guidance in the church. We highly recommend that groups experience the twenty-eight-week foundational program before using *The Way of Discernment*. The group would then be (1) grounded in the basic spiritual practices from which discernment arises, such as scriptural meditation and listening prayer, and (2) bonded in the kind of mutual trust that best facilitates their full engagement with this small-group process.

If you use this resource without benefit of the foundational program, we strongly urge you to arrange an additional meeting, after the Preparatory Meeting and before Week 1, simply to let group members get acquainted through sharing their spiritual autobiographies or personal stories and why this topic drew each member to participate. Experiencing this resource may also stimulate thirst in your group for a longer-term formational experience in community that the twenty-eight-week foundational resource could help facilitate.

About the Resource and Process

Like all resources in the Companions in Christ series, *The Way of Discernment* has two primary components: (1) individual reading and daily exercises throughout the week in the Participant's Book, and (2) a weekly two-hour meeting based on directions in the Leader's Guide. The Participant's Book has a weekly article that introduces new material and five daily exercises to help participants reflect on their lives in light of the article's content. These exercises help participants move from *information* (knowledge about) to *experience* (knowledge of). An important part of this process involves keeping a personal notebook or journal in which participants record reflections, prayers, and questions for later review and for reference at the weekly group meeting. The time commitment for daily exercises is twenty to thirty minutes. The weekly meeting includes time for reflecting on the past week's article and exercises, for moving into deeper experiences of spiritual growth, and for engaging in group experiences of worship.

The material in *The Way of Discernment* includes a preparatory meeting, followed by ten weekly sessions. Following is a brief overview of the content of the sessions.

Week 1. *The Beckoning of Discernment:* Considering discernment as deep desire, received gift, and intentional path.

Week 2. *The Heart of Discernment:* Acknowledging God as the source of discernment, the Holy Spirit's role in the leading of Christ, and the need to expand our ideas of God's will.

Week 3. *Fruits as Touchstones:* Exploring anticipated and actual fruits of a decision, and inward and outward expressions of fruitfulness, as key criteria for sound discernment.

Week 4. *Core Identity as Touchstone:* Rooting ourselves in the spiritual truth of our beloved identity in God, and staying grounded in that core identity, as foundations for discerning God's will.

Week 5. *Growing in the Gift:* Opening ourselves to greater receptivity and response to the gift of discernment through spiritual disciplines, questions, and willingness.

Week 6. *In the Hard Places:* Acknowledging the struggles of discernment, discovering the gifts of waiting, learning how to live amid desolation, and identifying consolation.

Week 7. *Communal Discernment—Beginnings:* Fostering a healthy climate for communal discernment, embracing basic steps for seeking God's will together, and introducing models for group help with individual discernment.

Week 8. Communal Discernment—Going Farther: Exploring various approaches to corporate discernment: living with a long-term question, using images and silence in gatherings, and following key steps through more complex situations.

Week 9. *Elements of Perpetual Challenge:* Acknowledging the challenge of following God's will, accepting the prophetic dimension of the call, and faithfully bearing the cross.

Week 10. The All-Encompassing Assurance: Receiving through scripture and sacrament the great assurance of Jesus' presence with us "to the end of the age."

The Companions in Christ Web Site

The Companions in Christ Web site provides a wealth of information for group leaders and participants. The site includes responses to frequently asked questions, tips for leading formational groups, downloadable resources for group leaders, and information on the entire Companions in Christ family of resources. Visit www.CompanionsInChrist.org.

The Role of the Small-Group Leader

Leading a group for spiritual formation differs in many ways from teaching a class. The most obvious difference is in your basic goal as group leader. In a class, you generally want to convey particular facts or interpretations and encourage discussion of ideas. You can gauge your success at the end of a class by how well participants demonstrate some grasp of the information. In a group for spiritual formation, your goal is to enable spiritual growth in each group member. You work in partnership with the Holy Spirit, who alone brings about transformation of the heart. Here gaining wisdom is more important than gaining knowledge, and growing in holiness is more important than either knowledge or wisdom. Success, if that word has any meaning in this context, will be evident over months and even years in the changed lives of group members.

Classes tend to be task-oriented. Groups for spiritual formation tend to be more process-oriented. Even though group members will have done common preparation in reading and daily exercises, group reflections may move in directions you do not expect. You will need to be open to the movement of the Holy Spirit and at the same time discerning of the difference between following the Spirit's lead and going off on a tangent. Such discernment requires careful, prayerful listening—a far more important skill for a small-group leader than talking.

Finally, classes tend to focus on external sources, such as the Bible, theological books, films, or current events. In contrast, spiritual formation groups focus more on internal realities: personal faith experience in daily life and spiritual practice. Group members seek to understand and receive the grace and revelation of God. When participants reflect on a scripture text, the basis for group interaction is not "What did the author intend to say to readers of that time?" but "How does this passage speak to my life or illuminate my experience?" Group discussions focus sharing insights, not on debating ideas. As leader, you will model such personal sharing with your group because of your involvement in all aspects of the Companions experience. Your leadership here differs substantially from that of a traditional adult class teacher. As a participant-leader you will read the articles and complete the daily exercises along with everyone else, bringing your responses to share with the group. You will lead by offering your honest reflections and by enabling group members to listen carefully to one another and to the Spirit in your midst.

Leading a spiritual formation group requires particular qualities. Foremost among these are **patience** and **trust**. You need patience to allow sessions to unfold as they will. Spiritual formation is a lifelong process. Identifying visible personal growth in group members over the course of *The Way of Discernment* may be difficult. It may take a while for participants to adjust to the purpose and style of the formational group process. As a group leader, **resolve to ask questions with no "right" answers in mind** and to encourage group members to talk about their own experiences. Setting an example of sharing your own experience rather than proclaiming abstract truths or talking about the experiences of other well-known Christians will accelerate this shift from an informational to a formational process. Trust that the Holy Spirit will indeed help group members see or hear what they really need. You may offer what you consider a great insight to which no one responds. If the group needs it, the Spirit will bring it around again at a more opportune time. Susan Muto, a modern writer on spiritual formation, often says that we need to "make space for the pace of grace." There are no shortcuts to spiritual growth. Be patient and **trust the Spirit.**

Listening is another critical quality for a leader of a spiritual formation group. This does not mean simply listening for people to say what you hope they will say so you can reinforce them. Listen for what is actually going on in participants' minds and hearts, which may differ from what you expect after reading the material and doing the weekly exercises yourself. While listening, jot down brief notes about themes that surface. Does sharing seem to revolve around a certain type of experience? Is a hint of direction or common understanding emerging—a clue to God's will or at least a shared sense of meaning for the group? What do you hear again and again? What action might group members take together or individually to respond to an emerging sense of call?

A group leader also needs to be **accepting**. Accept that group members may have spiritual perceptions quite unlike yours and that people often see common experiences in different ways. Some may be struck by an aspect that did not impress you at all, while others may be left cold by dimensions that really move you. As you model acceptance, you help foster acceptance of differences within the group. In addition to accepting differences, you will need to **accept lack of closure**. Group meetings rarely tie up all loose ends in a neat package. Burning questions will be left hanging. You can trust the Spirit to bring resolution in time, if resolution is needed. Also be prepared to accept people's emotions along with their thoughts and experiences. Tears, fears, joy, and anger are legitimate responses along this journey. One important expression of acceptance is permission-giving. **Permit group members to grow and share at**

their own pace. Let them know in your first meeting that while you encourage full participation in every part of the process, they are free to opt out of anything that makes them feel uncomfortable. No one will be forced to share or pray without consent. "Where the Spirit of the Lord is, there is freedom" (2 Cor. 3:17).

It is important to avoid three common tendencies of small groups and their leaders:

1. *Fixing.* When someone presents a personal or theological problem, you may be tempted to find a solution or give your priceless advice. Problem solving generally makes you feel better. Perhaps it makes you feel wise or helps break the tension, but it rarely helps the other to grow. Moreover, you might prescribe the wrong "fix." If you have faced a similar problem, speak only from your own experience.

2. *Proselytizing.* You know what has brought you closer to God; naturally, you would like everyone to try it. You can offer your own experience to the group, but trying to convince others to follow your path is spiritually dangerous. Here is where your knowledge and wisdom come into play. Teresa of Ávila wrote that if she had to choose between a director who was spiritual and one who was learned, she would pick the learned one. The saint might be able to talk only about his or her own spiritual path. The learned one might at least recognize another person's experience from having read about it. Clarifying and celebrating someone else's experience is far more useful than urging others to try to follow your way.

3. *Controlling.* Many of us are accustomed to filling in silence with comment. You may be tempted to think you should have an appropriate response to whatever anyone says—you may tend to dominate and control the conversation. Here again, patience and listening are essential. Do not be afraid of silence. Being comfortable with silence allows you to be a relaxed presence in the group. If you cannot bear a long silence, break it with an invitation for someone (perhaps one who has been quiet so far) to share a thought, feeling, or question, rather than with a comment of your own.

If this style of leadership seems challenging or unfamiliar, consider attending a leader training event for *Companions in Christ.* While leadership training is not required, it is recommended and encouraged.

Expectations for the Opening and Sharing Insights Sections of Meetings

In the first hour of your group's weekly meeting, the first step is prayerful centering in God's presence. Invoking the Holy Spirit's guidance is especially important in the Opening (see "A General Outline for Group Meetings," pp. 18–20).

The Sharing Insights portion of the meeting allows participants to discuss their insights, questions, and experiences related to the reading and daily exercises. Encourage members to bring their journals to refresh their memories of the week's exercises. As leader, you will generally begin with your own reflections, setting the tone for the group. Speak briefly (2–3 minutes) in order to allow ample time for others to share. Above all, specifically relate one of your responses to a daily exercise. If your sharing is general or abstract, other participants will be less likely to share personal experiences. Your initial offering in this part of the meeting is one of your most important roles as a group leader. Consider carefully each week what you would like to say, remaining mindful of the role your words can play in establishing group trust and the serious intent in this part of the meeting.

You may also describe and model for the group an approach sometimes called "sharing to the center." The Christ candle set in the midst of the group affirms that Christ is truly the center of all that the group members do and say in the meeting. The living Christ, through the presence of the Holy Spirit, mediates personal sharing. Therefore, participants can share with one another in God's presence by visually focusing on the candle. This focus lessens the need for constant eye contact with other participants, often making it easier to reveal honest personal responses. The practice also helps the group to sense that God is truly the one with healing answers and guiding solutions, not us.

Your main job during the Sharing Insights time is to listen deeply and encourage members to listen fully to one another. Listen for indications of divine presence, and for themes—similar experiences that suggest a general truth about the spiritual life, common responses to the readings that might indicate a word God wants the group to hear, or insights that might offer practical help as participants try to hear and respond to the Spirit's call. Take notes so you can name these things. In time, you will invite other members to share themes or patterns they can identify, which slowly develops their capacity to discern. Listen, too, for key differences in participants' experiences, and affirm the variety of ways God speaks to each of us.

When you notice participants falling into the habit of fixing, controlling, or proselytizing, gently remind them to share from their own experiences or responses. The same guidance applies if a participant mentions someone else as an example, whether within or beyond the group. Nothing destroys group trust more quickly than exposing confidences.

By establishing up front some ground rules for group sharing, you may avoid problems. In the Preparatory Meeting, you will explain the various components of each week's meeting. Discuss the nature of this sharing time and establish your group's basic ground rules. Here are some suggestions:

- Speak only for yourself about beliefs, feelings, and responses.

- Respect and receive what others offer, even if you disagree.

- Listen more than talk. Avoid "cross talk"—interrupting, speaking for others, or trying to fix another person's problems.

- Honor the different ways God works in individuals.

- Do not be afraid of silence. Use it to listen to the Spirit in your midst.

- Maintain confidentiality. What is shared in the group stays in the group. If spouses or close friends are in the same group, they will want to establish (outside of meeting time) mutually agreeable boundaries to their personal sharing in the group.

- Recognize that all group members have permission to share only what and when they are ready to share.

- Group members have permission to opt out of a process but not to belittle it aloud.

You may want to add to this list before you discuss it with the group.

A few minutes before the scheduled end of the Sharing Insights time, state aloud any themes you have noted—a summary report on what you have heard, not a chance to get in the last word. Make it fairly brief: "I noticed that several of us were drawn to a particular passage. I wonder if God is trying to call our attention to something here." This is a time for summarizing and tying together themes that have already surfaced. After a few meetings, ask others in the group to identify themes or patterns they notice.

Finally, you may want to close this part of the session with prayer for the deepening of particular insights, for the ability to follow through on themes or guidance you have heard, for God's leading on questions left open, or for particular situations that have been mentioned. Or you may prefer to invite all group members who are willing to offer simple sentence prayers of their own. Pay attention to the time so you can bring sharing to a close and have time for the summary and prayer.

A General Outline for Group Meetings

Weekly group meetings will typically follow the outline explained below. Within the outline are two overall movements: one emphasizes sharing insights from the week's reading and daily exercises; the other develops an experiential understanding of spiritual practice or process. The first movement, Sharing Insights, has just been described. The second part of the meeting, Deeper Explorations, may expand on ideas contained in the week's reading, offer practice in related spiritual exercises, or give participants time to reflect on the personal or congregational implications of what they have learned. It may at times include a brief look forward to the coming week.

Both movements are intended as times for formation. The first focuses on group members' personal responses to the weekly reading and exercises and deep listening to one another. The second focuses on expanding and deepening the week's theme experientially. Some participants may respond more readily to one part of the meeting than the other. For example, one person may eagerly participate in the Sharing Insights time but be reticent to join a group process for Deeper Explorations. Another person may have little to say during Sharing Insights but receive great energy and joy from participating in experiential learning. Such variations of response may reflect differing personality types, circumstances, or life stages. Be patient, accepting, and encouraging of the fullest level of participation each group member can offer.

Consider carefully the setting for your group meetings. An adaptable space enhances your options for group process. One helpful arrangement is a circle of comfortable chairs. Participants may need a surface for writing or drawing at times. Since the group will sometimes break into pairs or triads, plenty of room to separate is also important. Choose a meeting space that is relatively quiet and peaceful.

A sacred visual focus for the group is important, especially for opening and closing worship times. You may create this focus in whatever way you choose. Each week includes suggestions for symbols that would be thematically appropriate to add to the tablecloth and Christ candle on a small, centrally placed table.

OPENING (10–15 MINUTES)

This brief time of worship gives group members a chance to quiet down and prepare inwardly for the group session. This Leader's Guide includes specific suggestions for simple worship each week, but you can develop your own pattern of centering. Possibilities for this opening worship include (1) singing a hymn or listening to a song; (2) silence; (3) lighting a candle; (4) a scripture, poem, or other reading; (5) individual or group prayer, planned or extemporaneous; and (6) a blessing.

SHARING INSIGHTS (40–45 MINUTES)

The content for this part of the meeting comes from participants' responses to the weekly reading and the five daily exercises they completed since the last meeting. If members fail to read the chapter or skip the daily exercises, they will be left out. If too many come unprepared, the group process simply will not work. A distinctive feature of *The Way of Discernment* is the inclusion of an additional sharing process around the "question of the week" at the beginning of the Sharing Insights time. Please review this process carefully, as it introduces a new element and shortens the time available for shared responses to other daily exercises.

BREAK (10 MINUTES)

Group break time serves important physical, mental, and relational purposes. It also offers a chance for snacking if you choose to do that. If so, arrange for someone to provide simple snacks. Do not neglect this break time, and be sure to take a break yourself as a leader.

DEEPER EXPLORATIONS (45 MINUTES)

This part of the meeting helps participants explore in greater depth the weekly theme, generally through scriptural meditation, creative process, personal reflection, and sharing. Group members first reflect on how God's call to a holy life is expressed and what God yearns for in our world. Then they come back to how the Spirit may be inviting them to help reshape church life in relation to the world God loves. You may need to help the group understand this as a valid subject for any congregational small group to explore, even if few/none of your group members hold leadership roles at present. The relationship of this small-group experience to its wider faith community is of vital concern in all Companions resources, whose purpose is not merely to enrich individuals but to help transform church cultures toward spiritual practice and discernment. Resembling the experiential part of a spiritual retreat in miniature, this segment of the meeting requires thoughtful preparation if you are to guide it comfortably. Review the leader material early in the week prior to the meeting so that you have time to think through the process, complete any preparation, and gather materials.

CLOSING (10 MINUTES)

As it began, the meeting ends with a brief time of worship following specific suggestions. In *The Way of Discernment*, several elements of the Closing repeat to form a pattern over time, in the service of deepening your group's capacity to discern patterns of grace and call. You may wish to include elements not suggested, such as asking for prayer requests and establishing prayer partners over the course of the ten weeks.

Music Matters

Song or hymn selections for the Opening and Closing times need careful consideration. Review the hymnals or songbooks available to you, and look for singable tunes with thematically appropriate words. If your group sings reluctantly, locate recorded music to play and invite participants to sing along or simply enjoy listening.

This Leader's Guide occasionally suggests songs. Some come from *The Faith We Sing* (TFWS), a songbook from Abingdon Press (a CD with musical accompaniment for every song is also available). Other suggested songs are found in the new *Upper Room Worshipbook* (URW; order through www.upperroom.org/bookstore). Both of these recommended resources are ecumenical, with songs representing several worship styles. *The Upper Room Worshipbook* includes many familiar hymns with fresh words; sung psalms; and global songs, including Taizé chants. Consider these music resources, while recognizing that each group has access to different songbooks and may have its own preference. Traditional hymns are referenced from *The United Methodist Hymnal* (UMH), though they can be found in many other hymnals.

Tips for Leading The Way of Discernment

As leader, you have the responsibility to prepare yourself conscientiously and spiritually before each meeting. Review the entire scope of this resource before you begin, so you have a clear sense of how it builds thematically and what your group can expect as it progresses through these ten weeks. You may wish to suggest two meetings to cover some topics, in order to relax the pace and benefit more fully from the experience. (Some groups have decided to take two weeks for every chapter, engaging in the Opening and Sharing Insights one week and the Deeper Explorations and Closing the following week.) Notice that the final meeting will be about twenty minutes longer than usual; notify your group about this well ahead of time.

Be aware that you may not be able to experience each part of every meeting, depending on your group's size and way of engaging the material. You will need to be sensitive to the personality of your group and alert to participants' energy level. Relative to these, you may need to choose what to keep and what to lay aside in the Leader's Guide material. Some weeks you will find suggestions about what to cut and can do so in advance. Yet it is equally important to be alert to the promptings of the Holy Spirit while leading the meeting itself. You may choose to delete a process midway through the meeting, or to add a time of prayer spontaneously based on what has happened in the group. Learn to follow your intuition when you feel unsure of the direction to take, or seek the group's wisdom on how to proceed. Remember to trust the grace of the Spirit in your midst!

You are free to adapt your approach as you believe it will best fit your group's need. For example, if your group has not been together before and lacks the bonds of mutual trust, or if group members seem reluctant to share personal thoughts early in the group's life, allow them to share in pairs or triads until they have built trust with one another. Or, in relation to sharing insights around the "question of the week," you might divide your group's journaling review on this question from their journaling review on the five daily exercises, so that the review immediately precedes each segment of sharing. (See Week 2, first part of Sharing Insights, p. 47, for the context of this suggestion.)

You are given the option of occasionally omitting the reflection process with the question of the week in order to allow more time for sharing around the daily exercises or engaging the Deeper Explorations. However, *please do not make this omission a general habit.* Giving the group regular opportunities to reflect on these longer-term questions affords them experience with a simple practice in discernment. Toward the end of this resource it should be evident that formulating fruitful questions to contemplate and pray with over time is itself a matter of discernment. Initial thoughts about the phrasing and meaning of a question can shift, clarify, and sharpen with time. Let the Spirit work with your group on shaping the questions that surface through these weeks together.

The purpose of the Companions in Christ series is to equip persons of faith with both personal and corporate spiritual life practices that will continue long beyond the time frame of any particular resource. Participants may continue certain disciplines on their own or carry some practices into their congregational life. Others may desire to continue meeting as a small group. As you guide your group through this journey, you may discover that certain practices or topics generate particular interest and energy. When the group expresses strong desire to go deeper into a particular topic or practice, take note of it. A number of possibilities exist for further small-group study and wider corporate practice beyond this resource. Some suggested resources are listed on pages 125–27 of the Participant's Book, and the appendix section on pages 117–139 in this guide offers several further approaches for personal and congregational use. The group will need to decide future directions toward the end of this experience.

Our prayer for you as a leader is that in the weeks ahead, the Spirit will guide you and your group deeper into the marvelous gift and practice of spiritual discernment. May your explorations lead you into greater union with the intentions of God and the joy of new energy for service that grows from listening prayer. May your companionship with Christ and one another be richly blessed!

Weekly Needs at a Glance

Review this Weekly Needs at a Glance list to familiarize yourself with items needed at *The Way of Discernment* Preparatory Meeting and the other weekly meetings. Knowing well in advance the items required will help you avoid last-minute stress. Many group leaders have found it helpful to keep a large basket with basic supplies ready for each meeting, to which distinctive items can be added or subtracted as needed.

Weekly Materials

ALL MEETINGS

- Christ candle (white pillar candle) or other central candle

- table, covered with a cloth

- matches or lighter

- hymnals, songbooks, or recorded music and playing equipment

- extra Bibles

- sheets of blank paper and pens or pencils (for those who forget their journals)

- bell or chime (to gently call the group back from personal reflection/cluster sharing)

- group ground rules developed during the Preparatory Meeting, printed on newsprint and posted in your meeting room

- newsprint or chalkboard/whiteboard with appropriate markers

- Candle Prayer, printed on newsprint and posted in your meeting room (or you may choose the alternate prayers printed in each week's Opening):

> *Light of Christ,*
> *shine on our path.*
> *Chase away all darkness*
> *and lead us to the heart of God.*
> *Amen.*

PREPARATORY MEETING

- copy of Participant's Book for each person (including you as leader)

- copies of the Companions *Journal* for those who may wish to purchase one

- marker and newsprint (or flipchart) with group ground rules written out in advance

- copy for each person of "Holy Listening Exercise" (p. 34) with "Review Questions" (p. 35) copied on reverse side

- "Prayers for Our Way of Discernment Group" card (at the back of this Leader's Guide)

- hymns or songs for Opening and Closing

WEEK 1: THE BECKONING OF DISCERNMENT

- copy for each participant of "Meditating with Proverbs 2:1-10" (p. 43)

- preprinted question for listening process on newsprint (p. 40)

- question of the week from Closing, written on a 3 by 5 card for each participant

WEEK 2: THE HEART OF DISCERNMENT

- an image of wholeness for worship focus (optional)

- drawing paper, colored pencils or crayons for Deeper Explorations

- question of the week from Closing, written on a 3 by 5 card for each participant

WEEK 3: FRUITS AS TOUCHSTONES

- symbol of fruitfulness for worship focus (optional)
- copy for each person of "Anticipated Fruits" personal reflection sheet (p. 59)
- question of the week from Closing, written on a 3 by 5 card for each participant

WEEK 4: CORE IDENTITY AS TOUCHSTONE

- symbol of our identity in God's love for worship focus (optional)
- copy for each person of "Finding Freedom to Be Alive in God" (p. 66)
- question of the week from Closing, written on a 3 by 5 card for each participant

WEEK 5: GROWING IN THE GIFT

- symbol of receptivity for worship focus (optional)
- preprint on newsprint or marker board (or create handout of) "Preconditions for Discernment" (p. 70)
- copy for each person of "Gestation Model of Personal Discernment" (p. 74)
- copy for each person of "Psalm 131" (p. 75)
- question of the week from Closing, written on a 3 by 5 card for each participant

WEEK 6: IN THE HARD PLACES

- symbol of waiting or consolation/desolation for worship focus (optional)
- masking tape or plastic adhesive (for use with newsprint during Deeper Explorations)
- newsprint and marker
- crayons or colored pencils
- question of the week from Closing, written on a 3 by 5 card for each participant

WEEK 7: COMMUNAL DISCERNMENT—BEGINNINGS

- symbol of listening for worship focus (optional)
- copy for each person of "Clearness Committee Description" (pp. 89–90)
- copy for each person of "Sample Questions for a Clearness Committee" (p. 91)*
- question of the week from Closing, written on a 3 by 5 card for each participant

*Note the possible need to brief a group member for his or her role in the Clearness Committee.

WEEK 8: COMMUNAL DISCERNMENT—GOING FARTHER

- symbol of prayer for worship focus (optional)
- copy for each person of "Discerning God's Prayer in Us for Another" (p. 99)
- question of the week from Closing, written on a 3 by 5 card for each participant

WEEK 9: ELEMENTS OF PERPETUAL CHALLENGE

- a cross for worship focus (optional)
- three columns with headings preprinted on newsprint or marker board (p. 103, under Deeper Explorations)
- blank 3 by 5 cards for each participant

WEEK 10: THE ALL-ENCOMPASSING ASSURANCE

- baptism and Communion symbols for worship focus (optional)
- visual image of five intersecting circles with words, as specified on page 107, preprinted on newsprint or marker board
- masking tape
- quote from Patricia Loring preprinted on newsprint or chalkboard/marker board
- copy for each person of "Liturgy for Discernment" (p. 135)

Preparatory Meeting

*T*his book directly addresses you, the leader, as it presents material for each group meeting. In places the Leader's Guide offers suggested words for you to speak as a way of introducing various sections to the group. Where this occurs, words are printed in bold typeface (such as the first item under "Set the context"). These words are only suggestions. Feel free to express the same idea in your own words or adapt as you deem necessary. Remember to speak at a deliberate pace. Whether giving instructions or offering prayers, not rushing your words helps communicate a sense of peace and grace.

When instructed to guide a reflection process, you will often see ellipses (...). These marks indicate pauses between your sentences to allow participants to ponder them. You will need to develop your own sense of timing in relation to the overall time frame for the guided meditation. Generally, twenty to thirty seconds are sufficient for each pause. In some cases, the text will recommend specific times for pauses.

The Leader's Guide assumes groups are new to the Companions in Christ resources and provides complete explanation of all aspects of the journey. For example, in this Preparatory Meeting participants carefully review the daily and weekly rhythm and are introduced to the printed resource. If your entire group has already experienced Companions, feel free to abbreviate familiar material and focus on distinctive aspects of this resource and your group's process. One exception is the "Holy Listening Exercise." A review of deep listening, so central to spiritual formation, can benefit even an experienced group. We strongly encourage leaders to include this exercise at the start of every Companions group.

PREPARATION

Prepare yourself spiritually. Read the introduction in this Leader's Guide with thorough attention. Review the introduction to your Participant's Book also, marking it so you can point to essential aspects of group process in your explanation after the opening worship time. Look over the Contents page in the Participant's Book so you can answer basic questions about weekly topics. Pray for your newly forming group and for each participant by name. If co-leading, pray with your leading partner. Ask that God will increase a discerning spirit in you and in each group member as together you embark on this spiritual journey.

Prepare materials and the meeting space.

- Set up chairs in a circle with a small center table, cloth, and Christ candle (white pillar candle). Make your meeting space inviting and visually attractive.

- Have a copy of the Participant's Book for each person and several copies of the Companions *Journal* for those who may wish to purchase one.

- You will need a marker and flipchart or newsprint with group ground rules written out in advance (see introduction, p. 18).

- Provide the card "Prayers for Our *Way of Discernment* Group" (in back of this Leader's Guide) for participants to sign.

- You will need copies for each participant of the handout "Holy Listening Exercise" with the accompanying "Review Questions" copied on the reverse side.

- Choose hymns/songs for the Opening and Closing, and secure hymnals/songbooks. You may also select recorded music to play. We particularly recommend *The Upper Room Worshipbook* (URW) for a splendid variety of songs, Taizé chants, and familiar hymns with fresh words. *The Faith We Sing* (TFWS) is also helpful.

Review the intent of this meeting: to gain a clear grasp of the purpose and process of *The Way of Discernment*; to provide opportunity to ask questions and express hopes for the journey; to begin getting acquainted within the group; and to review and adopt group ground rules.

OPENING (*20 minutes*)

Welcome all participants by name as they enter. Be sure each participant has a copy of *The Way of Discernment* Participant's Book and a journal or notebook.

Set the context.

- **This meeting will prepare us for a ten-week journey of exploration into a deeply important and timely spiritual practice, that of discernment.**

- Discernment comes to us as a natural fruit of spiritual reflection and prayer. As Christians, we grow in our capacity to discern the will of God by opening ourselves more and more to the grace and guidance of the Holy Spirit. That is precisely what we will be practicing over the next ten weeks together.

- Like all Companions in Christ resources, *The Way of Discernment* is a small-group experience in spiritual formation. The purpose of spiritual formation is to give the Spirit time and space to shape us into greater Christlikeness.

Provide a brief overview of the Preparatory Meeting.

— A chance for group members to introduce themselves
— Opening worship similar to what they will experience in each weekly meeting
— Discussion of the group process
— Discussion of group members' responsibilities
— An experience in "holy listening"
— Closing worship similar to what they will experience in each weekly meeting

Invite participants to introduce themselves.

- Ask them to say their name and a few words about what drew them to this group.

- As leader, model by introducing yourself first. Keep your comments brief and simple to encourage others to do likewise.

Join together in worship.

- Invite the group into a spirit of worship. Light the Christ candle, indicating you will begin each meeting this way to acknowledge the presence of the risen Lord in your midst. Offer words such as: **Living Christ, we light this candle trusting your true presence in our time together here. Open our minds and hearts to your spirit of grace and guidance as we begin to explore** *The Way of Discernment* **together.**

- Read Psalm 16:11. Allow a few moments of quiet to let people absorb the words. Say something to this effect: **Discernment is about finding the path of life and joy, the path on which we know God's presence and good gifts.**

- Read the verse a second time. Invite people to ponder silently what they most seek to learn through this small group. Allow a few minutes of quiet.

- Offer prayer with words like these:

  O God, in your presence there is indeed fullness of joy! Through Christ you reveal the path to your own heart and will. Through the Spirit you are willing to show us the way. Thank you for your faithful guidance. Open us to what you have in store through these coming weeks, in Jesus' name. Amen.

- Sing a song or hymn together. Suggestion: "Be Thou My Vision" (UMH #451)

PRESENT THE RESOURCES AND GROUP PROCESS *(10 minutes)*

Go over the introduction to the Participant's Book with group members so each person understands the basic process of reading, daily exercises, and journaling, as well as the outline for each group meeting. Participants need not read the whole introduction at this time, but encourage them to read it in full before the Week 1 meeting. Some items you will want to mention:

Basic flow of the week. Each participant reads the article for the week on Day 1 (the day after the group meeting) and works through the five daily exercises over Days 2 through 6. The group meets on Day 7. Encourage participants' faithfulness to the process. In preparation for the group meeting, suggest that after Daily Exercise 5 they read over their notebook or journal entries for that week.

Basic flow of the group meeting. Explain the various components: Opening, Sharing Insights, Deeper Explorations, and Closing. Summarize for the group the explanatory material found in "A General Outline for Group Meetings" on pages 18–20 of the introduction to this Leader's Guide.

Materials for each meeting. Ask members to bring their Bibles, Participant's Books, and journals to each meeting. Because use of the Bible is part of the daily exercises, encourage participants to use a favorite modern translation.

Time commitment. Explain that the weekly meeting requires two hours, and that in *The Way of Discernment* the final meeting (Week 10) will be 15–20 minutes longer than usual. The expected time commitment for each daily exercise is 20–30 minutes. Help participants see that this resource offers a way to build a daily habit of spiritual practice into our lives.

EXPLAIN PARTICIPANT RESPONSIBILITIES *(15 minutes)*

Emphasize the importance of each member's commitment to reading and daily exercises in making the group process work. If some members have not experienced this type of daily reflection or group interaction, they may need help in feeling comfortable with them. Remind participants: **One of the ways we listen to God is by putting our spiritual reflections into words. Throughout the week, we record these experiences in our journal. In the group meeting, we share from what we have recorded. Both processes offer clarity and new perspective.**

Present the process of journaling.
Note that some participants may already be experienced in journaling. Call the group's attention to pertinent points from the material on pages 10–11 of the Participant's Book introduction about the value of recording reflections in a journal or personal notebook. Assure them that the writing can be as informal and unstructured as they choose. Each person keeps notes that are most helpful for him or her, so the journal becomes a personal record of spiritual growth through the period this group works with the topic.

Consider the commitment of listening.
Group members also commit to listen to and value the words of others:

> **As companions together, we give full attention to what God is doing in the life of the one speaking. We learn to listen with our heart as well as our head and to create an accepting space in which all can freely explore their spiritual journeys.**

The group becomes a place for deep listening and trusting in God's guidance. Let your group know that developing listening skills is crucial to spiritual formation, and that later in this meeting everyone will have an opportunity to experience a practice called "Holy Listening."

DISCUSS COMMON GROUND RULES *(10 minutes)*

Ground rules are explained fully on pages 17–18 in the introduction. The basic rules suggested there should prove helpful, but you may wish to add something appropriate or allow group members to make suggestions. If all agree on these, add them to the list on newsprint for the group to see. Your goal is not a formal agreement but recognition of the basic rules essential for the group to deepen its faith and to mature as a community. These rules may also be understood as a covenant.

BREAK *(10 minutes)*

DEEPER EXPLORATIONS *(45 minutes)*

Introduce the "Holy Listening Exercise." (10 minutes)

- This exercise gives everyone a chance to practice prayerful or holy listening, the heart of spiritual friendship. Listening practice is essential to formational experience in all settings: formal or informal, one-on-one or in a group of any size.

- Give everyone the handout "Holy Listening Exercise" with "Review Questions" on the reverse side. Explain this paired process to the group as they read it, and respond to any questions. Point out that as an exercise, it will feel constrained by time limits.

- Assure the group that each person in a pair will have the opportunity to be both a listener and a speaker. After the first eight minutes, they will take two minutes to reflect on the review questions. Then they trade roles. At end of the second eight minutes, they again take two minutes to reflect with the review questions. During the last five minutes, they will compare their responses to those questions.

- For this exercise ask group members to pair with someone they don't know well. As leader, you can pair with someone if necessary, but you will still need to track the time; or assign an unpaired person to be a prayerful listener to a pair.

Practice holy listening in pairs. (30 minutes)

- Ask pairs to find space apart quickly so as to make the most of the time.

- Help participants honor the time by ringing a bell or calling out the time after each eight-minute period, and by reminding them to take two minutes to reflect on the review questions. Alert the participants to switch roles at the close of this reflection time.

- After the second listening session and review, encourage each pair to compare notes on their experience for five minutes.

[You can allow another minute for each review, as some will need more time to consider these questions than others.]

Gather as a group. (5 minutes)

- Call pairs back into the group to share what they've learned about holy listening.

- Close with this affirmation: **There is no greater gift one person can give to another than to listen deeply from the heart.**

CLOSING *(10 minutes)*

Invite the group to a time of quiet reflection. **What are your hopes for the time ahead of us as companions in Christ? . . . What are your anxieties about these next weeks together? . . . Commit both your hopes and fears to God now in silent prayer. . . .**

Offer a brief word of prayer, asking that all might be able to offer hopes and release concerns into God's gracious hands. End with thanksgiving for each person and for God's good purposes in bringing this group together.

Close with a song or chant. Suggestion: "Take, O Take Me As I Am" (URW #441)

Explain the purpose of the "Prayers for Our Way of Discernment Group" card, and invite each person to sign his or her first name. Remind members of the assignment to read the article for Week 1 and work through one exercise each day afterward, recording thoughts in their journals. Be sure participants know the location and time of the next meeting and any special responsibilities (such as helping arrange the worship focus table or bringing snacks).

Holy Listening Exercise

Spiritual direction takes place when two people agree to give their full attention to what God is doing in one (or both) of their lives and seek to respond in faith.

—Eugene Peterson, *Working the Angles*

The purpose of this exercise is for participants to practice holy listening in pairs.

As the Speaker

Receive your chance to speak and be heard as an opportunity to explore an aspect of your faith you have struggled with during the past week. Remember, you and your friend meet in the company of God, who is the true guiding presence of this time together.

As the Listener

Practice listening with heart as well as head. Create a welcoming, accepting space in which the other person may explore freely his or her journey in your presence and the presence of God. Be natural, but be alert to your habitual or anxious needs to analyze, judge, counsel, fix, teach, or share your own experience. Try to limit your speech to gentle questions of clarification and honest words of encouragement.

Be prayerful as you listen, paying attention to the Spirit even as you listen to the holy mystery of the person before you.

When appropriate and unintrusive, you might ask your partner to explore simple questions such as:

- Where did you experience God's grace or presence in the midst of this time?

- Do you sense God calling you to take a step forward in faith or love? Is there an invitation here to explore?

How to Begin and End the Conversation

- Decide who will be listener first, and begin with moment of silent prayer.

- Converse for eight minutes; then pause for two minutes so each may respond in silence to the appropriate "Review Questions" on the reverse side.

- Trade roles and converse for eight minutes more; then pause again to respond to remaining review questions.

- Use the last five minutes to compare notes on your experiences and responses to the review questions.

Review Questions

FOR THE LISTENER

1. When were you most aware of God's presence (in you, in the other person, between you) in the midst of the conversation?

2. What interrupted or diminished the quality of your presence to God or to the other person?

3. What was the greatest challenge of this experience for you?

FOR THE SPEAKER

1. What was the gift of the conversation for you?

2. What in the listener's manner helped or hindered your ability to pay attention to your life experience and God's presence in it?

3. When were you most aware of God's presence (in you, in the other person, or between you) in the midst of the conversation?

Week 1

The Beckoning of Discernment

PREPARATION

Prepare yourself spiritually. Review the introduction to this Leader's Guide, paying particular attention to "Role of the Small-Group Leader" and "Expectations for the Opening and Sharing Insights Sections of the Meetings." Read the article for Week 1; reflect on each daily exercise and journal responses, noting the suggested order of sharing responses to exercises in the Sharing Insights time. Pray that as leader you will be wide open to the Holy Spirit's guiding presence throughout this meeting. Pray for each participant and for the group as a whole, that they may recognize the need for—and desire the gift of—discernment.

Prepare materials and the meeting space.

- As you prepare for each meeting, refer to Weekly Needs at a Glance (beginning on p. 23 of this guide). Review items listed under All Meetings and under Week 1.

- Consider how you will arrange the meeting room for comfort, practicality, and beauty. Arrange chairs in a circle or around a table. Include a small area as a worship focus with a cloth, Christ candle, and perhaps a small icon or flowers. Feel free to add symbols relating to each week's theme. For example, this week you might bring a heart (to represent desire), a picture of a path, and a small gift-wrapped box.

- Post the group's ground rules in a visible place, and the Candle Prayer if you choose to introduce it (see p. 24).

- Make sufficient copies of the reflection sheet "Meditating with Proverbs 2:1-10."

- Secure a bell or chime to call pairs/triads back to the larger group.

- Write the question for the Deeper Explorations listening process on newsprint so you can turn to it as needed. Write the weekly question from the Closing on 3 by 5 cards, one for each participant, including yourself: "Where in the world around me do I see the need for discerning God's wisdom?"

- Review the Weekly Meeting so you are thoroughly familiar with it and can lead without reading everything from the book.

- Select songs to sing/recorded music to play for Opening and Closing.

Review the intent of this meeting: to identify an aspect of divine wisdom we currently seek in our lives, and to begin the practice of listening for the Spirit's guidance.

OPENING (10 MINUTES)

Welcome participants personally as they enter. Try to minimize gathering banter by creating a welcome sense of peace where people can quiet themselves, shedding busyness and stress. Encourage punctuality by starting within few minutes of the stated start time (if you have a majority of the group present). With a smile and welcoming gesture, invite latecomers to enter and find their place. Simply keep going with the Opening process.

Set the context.

We are beginning a wonderful new venture: ten weeks of learning and practicing the art of spiritual discernment. In our first six weeks together, we will focus on personal discernment before turning to corporate practices. We start this week by considering what situations in our current lives we seek God's wisdom for. Then we'll begin the practice of listening for the Spirit's guidance through prayerful, openhearted meditation on a key question.

Light the Christ candle in your midst, saying words like these:

> We light this candle to remind us that the risen Lord, Jesus Christ, is present with us now, at the very center of our meeting here and at the center of our hearts. We also remember that the illumination of the Holy Spirit is the source of all discernment and wisdom in our lives, both individually and together.

Invite participants to listen as you read a scripture passage; ask them to pay attention to any word or phrase that especially draws their attention and to ponder it. Read Proverbs 2:1-10 without rushing.

Invite the group into silent prayer for guidance over the course of this journey. After a minute of quiet, offer a brief prayer or pray the Lord's Prayer together.

Sing or listen to a song/chant of your choosing. Suggestion: "Listen" (URW #416)

Offer a brief blessing such as: **May the Lord send us the gift of the Holy Spirit to guide and inspire these hours together. In Jesus' name, Amen.**

SHARING INSIGHTS (45 MINUTES)

During the next forty-five minutes, participants will identify and speak of ways they have experienced God's presence this week. Key to this sharing are insights and experiences in response to the week's reading and daily exercises.

- Ask group members to briefly review their journal entries in response to this week's article and the daily exercises.

- Following the review, encourage everyone to attend to God's presence in the group, and to what the Spirit may be saying through one another's words/experiences.

- Invite sharing to begin with a focus on Exercise 3 and practices/principles we may already know and bring to our time together. As leader, set the tone by offering your own response first, modeling honesty and brevity.

- Move to sharing around Exercises 4–5, identifying memories, experiences, and images related to discernment. Try to save time for those who may be ready to share responses to Exercise 1, alert to the likelihood that some group members may not feel prepared for such personal sharing in the first few weeks.

- During the last five minutes, invite participants to reflect on this sharing time and notice any common themes/impressions that might offer clues to the Spirit's guiding grace for the group.

- Note these in your own journal so you can track themes/impressions over the course of your ten weeks together and remind the group of things they notice.

BREAK (10 MINUTES)

DEEPER EXPLORATIONS (45 MINUTES)

Explore our need for personal discernment, and ponder practices that can help us find direction

Guide a reflection exercise with a Proverbs passage. (20 minutes)

- Hand out the reflection sheet "Meditating with Proverbs 2:1-10" and explain the process: ten minutes to reflect personally; another ten minutes to share with one or two others in the group. Any who finish the reflection sheet in fewer than ten minutes may look for someone else who is ready to share.

- Allow participants to find their own space in the room and respond to questions on the sheet. Fill out your own sheet as well, but keep track of timing.

- After ten minutes, invite shared responses in pairs/triads spread around the room or nearby halls. (If your group prefers to stay together, the sharing time will take longer, and you will need to decide whether to cut or adapt the second group process below.)

- Call the group back together with a bell or chime.

Lead the group through the simple process of listening to a question. (15 minutes)

The intent is to give participants a chance to listen for God's leading, first within themselves and then collectively, and to begin to sense where this leading may be taking them. The process works best for groups of three to six persons, so please brief a second leader if your group is larger than six, and divide into two groups. Explain the basic idea to participants:

During the next fifteen minutes, we will enter a process of listening deeply to a question, both individually and together. Please understand that this is not a time to discuss ideas but rather to share insights. The purpose is not to offer commentary, either on your own words or those of others. The purpose is to listen deeply to what is in our hearts, and to what God may be saying in and through us.

- Invite your group into quiet, opening to the presence of God in your midst.

- After a minute or so, invite participants to reflect prayerfully on the following question: **When I seek God's wisdom, what simple practice helps me most?** Pause and repeat the question.

- After another minute of silence, ask participants to let their inward answer to the question condense into a single phrase or sentence.

- Then gently invite each person to: (1) speak the phrase or sentence that has come to them, without elaboration; (2) listen prayerfully to the words each person offers.

- After all have spoken, invite participants into silence to listen to the echoes of their words. What resonates in their minds and hearts?

- As the group continues in silence, ask them to consider quietly what theme or voice they may be hearing beneath or through the words they have shared aloud.

- After another minute of silence, ask participants to share these deeper themes. Allow two or three minutes for this second round of sharing. (You or someone in the group might wish to capture key phrases on paper as people speak, and perhaps create a group prayer from them.)

- Acknowledge that new understandings may just be emerging, and invite the group back into quiet. Close with a simple prayer of thanks for fresh insights that have arisen (or with prayer created from the group's words/phrases).

Review the experience. (10 minutes)
[If the group has been divided, come back together.]

- Invite participants to reflect on their experience of the quiet, the listening, the simplicity of speaking just a few words or sentences, and the insights that may have begun to emerge from this prayerful listening.

- Name what you have just done as one simple way to begin discerning God's presence and guidance. Assure group members that they will have more opportunity to practice this way of listening to a question over the next several weeks. Encourage them to stay open to further answers that may surface over time to this question.

CLOSING (10 MINUTES)

Sing a song of gratitude and praise to God.

Give everyone a question to pray with over the coming week, written on a 3 by 5 card: "Where in the world around me do I see the need for discerning God's wisdom?" Invite participants to place the card in a visible location (bathroom mirror, car dashboard, computer monitor) where they will see it several times a day.

This kind of question (called the question of the week) will recur in our Closing each week, because living with an open-ended question over a period of time offers one very helpful path toward discernment. Please take just three to five minutes a day to reflect on the question and jot down responses that come to you, maybe just before or after the daily reflection exercise, or whenever you feel inspired. There's no need for a fixed or final answer; just let responses emerge and deepen over the days. At our next meeting you'll have an opportunity to share your responses.

Enter a time of silent gratitude; then invite one-sentence prayers.

Announce the time/date/location of your next meeting. Remind everyone of the importance of reading the article and doing the daily exercises—both for the integrity of the group meeting and the growth of each participant. This is a wonderful opportunity to build daily spiritual practice into our lives and to support each other in doing so.

Offer a closing benediction, perhaps in the words of 2 Timothy 4:22.

Meditating with Proverbs 2:1-10

1. Where in your life now do you "cry out for insight, and raise your voice for understanding" (v. 3)?

2. How have you searched for this understanding "as for hidden treasures" (v. 4)?

3. When do you believe you *have* received the gift of wisdom, knowledge, and understanding in some way that has significantly guided you?

Week 2

The Heart of Discernment

PREPARATION

Prepare yourself spiritually. Review "The Role of the Small-Group Leader" (p. 14) in the introduction. Read the article for Week 2, reflect on each daily exercise, and journal your responses. Pray that as leader you will be open to the Holy Spirit's gently directing presence throughout this meeting. Pray for each participant and for the group as a whole to recognize the real presence of Christ and understand more deeply the true nature of God's will for us.

Prepare materials and the meeting space.

- As you prepare for each meeting, refer to Weekly Needs at a Glance (beginning on p. 23). Review items listed under All Meetings and under Week 2.

- Consider how to arrange your meeting room for comfort, practicality, and beauty. Arrange chairs in a circle or around a table. Include a small area as a worship focus with a cloth, Christ candle, and any symbol representing the theme of this week—perhaps a depiction of the Peaceable Kingdom or another image of wholeness, such as a cathedral rose window or labyrinth.

- Post the group ground rules and Candle Prayer (if you use it) in a visible place.

- Select songs/recorded music for the Opening and Closing.

- Review the Weekly Meeting so you are thoroughly familiar with it and can lead without reading everything from the book.

- Collect drawing paper and colored pencils/crayons for the Deeper Explorations.

- Write the question of the week from the Closing on 3 by 5 cards for everyone.

- If your group is larger (9–12 persons), choose which of the two processes in Deeper Explorations you believe would most benefit the group. This way, members will not feel rushed and can fully engage in the experience. If you choose the first process (the question about God's will), divide your group in half and brief an additional group leader in advance.

- Even a small to midsize group (5–8 persons) may benefit from taking more time and moving deeply into a single experience for the Deeper Explorations. If you decide to offer both experiences, however, groups of six to eight still need to divide for the listening process in order to leave adequate time for the guided prayer.

- If you will lead the guided prayer in Deeper Explorations, practice timing your words so they feel spacious. If the guided prayer is the only process you will use, expand the timing and encourage people to respond to the meditation with sketched images/colors. You can also give more time to group debriefing of the experience.

- *Options:* If you elect a single process for the Deeper Explorations, you might wish to make a take-home handout of the other experience (turn the guided prayer into a personal prayer option, or the question about God's will into a journal exercise). This will entail some extra preparation on your part. An alternative would be to shorten the Deeper Explorations time frame, lengthen the Closing, and use an abbreviated form of the guided prayer process there before introducing the question of the week.

Review the intent of this meeting: to continue the practice of listening for the Spirit's guidance, and to revisit our notions of God's will.

OPENING (10 MINUTES)

Welcome participants personally as they enter. Again, begin as close to the stated start time as possible, welcoming latecomers with a smile and a nod to find their places.

Set the context.

Our first six weeks focus primarily on personal discernment, though there is always an element of group practice in what we do. This week we begin with the question we ended with last week: Where in the world around us do we perceive the need for discerning God's wisdom? Then we'll practice listening for the Spirit's guidance through prayerful meditation on another key question. Finally we will revisit, inwardly and together, our understanding of God's will. [Note: If you are using only one Deeper Explorations process, adapt the last two sentences as appropriate.]

Join together in worship.

- Light the Christ candle and recite the Candle Prayer, or offer words like these: **We light this candle to remind us of the presence and guidance of our Lord Jesus Christ, abiding at the center of our meeting and at the center of our lives. We remember that his presence comes to us through the gift of the Holy Spirit.**

- Read Romans 8:26-27 without rushing. After a pause, repeat verse 27. Invite participants to ponder the deep truth that the Spirit knows the will of God, just as God knows "the mind of the Spirit."

- Share this quote from author Gerald May: **"The real One who does the discerning is the Holy Spirit."**[1] Invite quiet reflection on the implications of this statement. You might softly repeat the statement after a few moments of silence.

- After a minute of quiet, offer a brief prayer or pray the Lord's Prayer together.

- Sing or listen to a song of your choosing. Suggestion: "Psalm 5 (Lead Me, Lord)" (URW #226).

SHARING INSIGHTS (45 MINUTES)

During the next forty-five minutes, participants will share how they have experienced God's presence and guidance this past week, drawing particularly on insights and experiences in response to the week's reading and daily exercises. Begin by considering the question from last week's Closing, as indicated below. If you find that most in the group have not spent time reflecting on this question, move ahead to the article and daily exercises.

- Ask group members to briefly review their journal entries in response to the week's article and daily exercises. Invite them also to review any reflections on the question of the week given at last meeting's Closing *(5 minutes)*.

- Encourage everyone to be attentive to God's presence in the group, and to what the Spirit may say through one another's words and experiences.

- Begin by guiding a brief reflection process *(10–15 minutes)* on last week's closing question, using the following guidelines:

Invite quiet, holding in awareness the question we have lived with over the week: **"Where in the world around me do I see the need for discerning God's wisdom?"**

- Ask participants to share, as they feel ready, just one or two answers that seem significant. Encourage prayerful listening to one another.

- After the sharing, return to quiet. Then invite any further perceptions that may have arisen as a result of hearing one another.

- Remind everyone that the point is not to reach final answers but to move toward a fuller understanding, under the Spirit's guidance.

- Continue with sharing from the week's reading and daily exercises. As leader, set the tone by offering your own response first, modeling honesty and brevity.

- During the last five minutes, invite participants to notice any common themes or impressions from this shared reflection time that might suggest a deeper message for the group as a whole.

- Note these in your own journal so you can track themes/impressions over these weeks together and remind the group of their noticings.

- Close with a brief prayer of thanks for emerging insights.

BREAK (10 MINUTES)

DEEPER EXPLORATIONS (45 MINUTES)

Revisiting our ideas about God's will

Set the context.

Now we will practice listening to a question in our group session together, rather than individually through the week. The *theme* of the question concerns God's will, which is central to all discernment. And the *practice* of listening offers us an approach or a path to discernment, as we will discuss further.

Lead the group through the process of listening to a new question. (20 minutes)

The intent is to give participants a chance to listen for God's leading, first within themselves and then collectively, and to begin to sense and sift where this leading may be taking them. Since this process works best with groups of three to six persons, please brief a second leader on the basic process if your group has more than six members.

- Invite your group into quiet, simply opening to the presence of God in your midst.

- After a minute or so, ask the following question: **When I think of the will of God, what image or color comes to mind?** Instruct group members not to overthink this question but to capture their immediate impression or gut instinct.

- Encourage them to take crayons or colored pencils and quickly sketch their image or draw their color, either in their journals or on larger sheets of paper if desired. You might suggest that those sketching an image use their nondominant hand so they can focus more on feeling tones and impressions than on drawing accuracy.

- After a minute or so, ask participants to condense into a few simple phrases or sentences what they would like to share with the group about their image/color.

- Then invite group members to (1) share what they choose to say about their image or color, without further elaboration; (2) listen prayerfully to each person.

- After all have shared, invite silence to hear the echoes or see the afterimages.

- As the group continues in silence, ask all to consider quietly: **What theme or Voice do you hear speaking through all that has been shared? What image encompasses or transcends all the images shared?**

- After a few minutes of silence, invite participants to share with one another what may be surfacing in answer to these questions.

- Allow up to five minutes for sharing. Acknowledge that new understandings may continue to emerge, and invite the group back into quiet. Close with a simple prayer of thanks for any fresh insights that have arisen.

Review the experience. (10 minutes)

- Invite participants to reflect on their experience of the quiet, the listening, the simplicity of speaking few words, the power of images and colors—any perceptions that may have emerged from this time.

- Name what you have done as one simple path toward discernment—in this case, around our perceptions of God's will. Personal discernment often involves distilling the essence of what we feel or hear inwardly in relation to a central question, and group discernment often involves distilling the deeper sense of what the group feels/hears together.

- Indicate that the group will have further opportunity to practice this form of discernment in weeks to come, as well as to learn other forms. Encourage participants to stay alert to new images or colors that may become associated with discernment over the course of these weeks together.

Guide the group in a prayer process: "Through Divine Eyes." (15 minutes)
This prayer allows participants to go deeper into their understanding of God's will through active imagination. Allow enough time for people to enter the imaginative process. Starting many phrases with the word *And* can help listeners stay in a meditative frame of mind with minimal interruption to the flow of images. [If you are focusing solely on this process with your group, expand the time frame and encourage members to reflect with colored pencils/crayons to express images and feelings.]

Set the context.

We often don't feel permission to imagine things from God's perspective. Yet the apostle Paul urges us to "put on" Christ (Col. 3:12–15, NASB) and to have the mind of Christ (Phil. 2:5). So in an act of faith, we are going to imagine viewing the world "through divine eyes" and see what illumination the Spirit may bring. We are not trying to play God here, but rather allowing the Holy Spirit to use our imaginations to expand our vision of reality. Feel free to write down thoughts or feelings that come to mind as you pray with your imagination. You may also wish to express your insights or feelings in color and images. (Indicate art supplies.)

Lead a guided prayer experience. (10 minutes)

1. Let's begin by entering prayerful quiet, resting with eyes closed. . . . Ask the Holy Spirit to direct your imagination. . . . And now imagine God looking out over the earth—in all its beauty and all its degradation—looking with deep love and compassion. . . . And imagine beginning to share in God's loving gaze. . . . Look now with God on the whole human family—in all its joy, pain, hope, and struggle. . . . And take time with God to love who you see, and to yearn over what you find. . . .

2. And as you continue sharing in God's loving gaze, begin to look on yourself.... What do you see through the eyes of God's love? ... what goodness? ... and hurt? ... and struggle? ... and possibilities? ...

3. And as you continue to look with God on yourself in a gaze of divine love, what do you begin to desire for yourself in the places of goodness? ... and in the hurt? ... and in the struggle? ... and in the possibilities? ...

4. Now gently withdraw from sharing God's loving gaze.... And simply continue in prayerfulness, asking, "What insight have I gained about God's will for the whole creation ... and the human family ... and for me? ..." And silently give thanks for any insights that have come.... Amen.

Reflect together on the process. (5 minutes)

As a group explore briefly what this experience was like. You might ask a few of the following questions: **Did it seem strange to imagine seeing through divine eyes? Was it intriguing or helpful? What insights did it yield? What questions did it raise?**

CLOSING (10 MINUTES)

Sing a song of your choosing. Suggestions:
    "Psalm 25 (To You, O Lord)"(URW #248) or
    "Psalm 23 (My Shepherd, You Supply My Need)" (URW #244)

Read Psalm 25:4-5. Allow a few moments of silence.

Introduce the question of the week, written on a 3 by 5 card: "How is the Spirit prompting, guiding, or beckoning me as I move through this week?" Invite group members to place their cards in a visible location (bathroom mirror, car dashboard, computer monitor) where they will see them several times a day.

Remind the group that this kind of question will recur in Closings for several weeks, offering a pathway to discernment over a period of time. Encourage participants to take three to five minutes each day to reflect prayerfully on the question and journal about it. The next meeting will offer opportunity to share responses during the Sharing Insights time.

Remind all of the date and time of your next meeting. Encourage the building of daily spiritual practice through reading the article and doing the daily exercises.

Offer a closing prayer:

O God, in you there is shelter and comfort.
Lead us in your truth and teach us your ways.
Your path is steady and sure.
Be our companion, our protector, and our deliverer. Amen.[2]

Week 3

Fruits as Touchstones

PREPARATION

Prepare yourself spiritually. If it would be helpful, review your role as small-group leader in the Leader's Guide introduction. Read the article for Week 3, reflect on the daily exercises, and journal your responses. Pray for openness to the guiding action of the Holy Spirit through this meeting. Pray for participants to recognize the fruits of the Spirit in their lives, and areas where they need further growth. Pray also that each group member will see how the fruits of the Spirit provide touchstones for discerning God's will.

Prepare materials and the meeting space.

- As you prepare for each meeting, refer to Weekly Needs at a Glance (beginning on p. 23 of this guide). Review items listed under All Meetings and under Week 3.

- Consider your meeting space. Arrange chairs in a circle, making sure there is enough space for participants to separate for personal reflection. Include in your worship focus area a cloth, Christ candle, and perhaps a cluster of grapes or other fruit in a bowl to symbolize the week's theme.

- Post the ground rules and Candle Prayer (if used) in a visible place.

- Make sufficient copies of the handout "Personal Reflection Sheet on Anticipated Fruits" for the Deeper Explorations.

- Review the Weekly Meeting so you are thoroughly familiar with it and can lead without simply reading from the book.

- Choose which process you will use for the Deeper Explorations, as you will be unable to do both in the time allotted. If your group is benefiting from the process of listening to a question, you might wish to build on this practice. You could even move the question of the week from Sharing Insights to Deeper Explorations if your group is small and you think there would be time for both. The reflection sheet could then be offered as a take-home exercise in case one of the daily exercises does not connect for a participant. On the other hand, you may feel your group would benefit more from a single experiential process with the reflection sheet.

- Write the question of the week from the Closing on 3 by 5 cards for everyone.

- Select songs/recorded music for the Opening and Closing.

Review the intent of this meeting: to continue the practice of listening for divine guidance, and to consider how the fruit of the Spirit offers touchstones for discerning God's will.

OPENING (10 MINUTES)

Welcome participants personally as they enter. Remember that beginning close to the stated start time will help participants develop the habit of arriving on time. Welcome latecomers with a smile and gesture to find their places.

Set the context.

This week we will continue listening deeply to key questions. First we'll share from the question we've been pondering this past week about how the Spirit has prompted, guided, or beckoned us. Then we'll listen as a group to a new key question. Finally we will practice anticipating the possible fruits of choices we might make, as an aid to learning discernment. [Note: Adapt these words according to the choices you have made about processes you will be leading.]

Join together in worship.

- Light the Christ candle, and recite the Candle Prayer or offer words like these: **We light this candle to remind us of the presence of Christ, abiding at the center of our meeting and of our lives. We remember that recognizing the fruit of his Spirit can guide our discernment of God's intentions for us.**

- Explain briefly the setting for the passage you are about to read: The king of Persia had been tricked by one of his courtiers into proclaiming an edict to kill all the Jews in his vast domain; his queen, Esther, was a Jew but had not revealed her identity as such to the king; Esther's adoptive father, Mordecai, had asked Esther to appeal to the king for the lives of her people, a dangerous tactic, since going to the king unbidden could mean death. [Feel free to expand this explanation.]

- Read Esther 4:12-16. After a pause, invite people to imagine standing in Esther's place. Say words like these: **The potential fruit of Esther's *inaction* was quite clear, whereas the fruit of *acting* on Mordecai's charge was less clear. It might lead to great good, or it might mean her fruitless death. Esther chooses an additional action on the part of her people before fulfilling Mordecai's request. Ponder silently how you think fasting relates to discernment in this story. . . . And how do you think fasting or any other spiritual discipline relates to discernment in our own lives? . . .**

- Invite brief prayers from the group, or offer your own. Close with the Lord's Prayer.

- Sing "Day by Day" or another song of your choosing.

- Offer this closing prayer from Richard of Chichester (c. 1198–1253):

   Thanks be to thee, O Lord Jesus Christ, for all the benefits which thou hast given us; for all the pains and insults which thou hast borne for us. O most merciful Redeemer, friend, and brother, may we know thee more clearly, love thee more dearly, and follow thee more nearly, for thine own sake. Amen.[1]

SHARING INSIGHTS (45 MINUTES)

During the next forty-five minutes, participants will share how they have experienced God's presence and guidance this past week, drawing especially on insights and experiences in response to the week's reading and daily exercises. Begin by considering the question from last week's Closing, as indicated below. If you find that most group members have not spent time reflecting on this question, move ahead to the article and daily exercises.

- Ask group members to briefly review their journal entries in response to the week's article and daily exercises. Invite them also to review any reflections on the question of the week given at last meeting's Closing. *(5 minutes)*

- Encourage everyone to be attentive to God's presence in the group, and to what the Spirit may say through one another's words.

- Begin by guiding a brief reflection process *(10–15 minutes)* on last week's closing question, using these guidelines:

> Invite quiet, holding in awareness the question we have lived with this past week: **How is the Spirit prompting, guiding, or beckoning me as I move through this week?**
>
> - Ask participants to share, as they feel ready, just one insight that seems significant. Encourage prayerful listening to one another.
>
> - After the sharing, return to quiet. Then invite any further perceptions that may have arisen as a result of hearing one another.
>
> - Note aloud any common themes and invite a moment of quiet gratitude.

- Continue with sharing from the week's reading and daily exercises. As leader, set the tone by offering your own response first, modeling honesty and brevity.

- In the last five minutes, invite all to reflect back over this time and identify any common themes/impressions that might suggest a deeper message for the group.

- Note these in your journal so you can track themes/impressions over the weeks together and remind group of their noticings.

- If sharing has been especially rich, take time to invite prayers of thanks and blessing.

BREAK (10 MINUTES)

DEEPER EXPLORATIONS (45 MINUTES)

Exploring the fruits of the Spirit in our lives

Option 1: Lead the group in listening together to a new question. (30 minutes)

Remember, the intent is to give participants a chance to listen for God's leading, first within themselves and then collectively; and to begin to sense where this leading may be taking them. This process works best for groups of three to six persons. Brief a second leader on the basic process if your group has more than six members.

- Invite your group into quiet, simply opening to the presence of God in your midst.

- After a minute or so, read John 13:34-35. Then ask: **When I think of the fruits that grow from a life rooted in Christ's love, what do I see, hear, or feel?** Repeat the question. Encourage participants to journal their responses *(allow 5 minutes).*

- Ask group members to condense their response into a few simple phrases/sentences. Allow a minute or so for them to consider and write what they will say.

- Then invite participants to (1) share their phrases/sentences without elaboration; (2) listen prayerfully to what each person offers.

- After all who choose to have shared, invite silence to hear the echoes of words spoken. Allow several minutes for this.

- As the group continues in silence, ask all to consider quietly, **What theme or Voice do you begin to hear speaking beneath and through what has been shared?**

- After a few minutes of silence, invite responses to this question. Allow time for sharing.

- Acknowledge that new understandings may continue to emerge, and invite the group back into quiet. Close with a short prayer of thanks for any insights that have arisen.

Review the experience. (10 minutes)
[If you have been in two groups, come back together.]

- Invite participants to reflect on their experience of the quiet, the listening, the speaking of few words, and the sensory impressions that may have occurred.

- Remind the group that you have just engaged in one rudimentary form of discernment. Encourage everyone to stay alert to new insights that may emerge over time in relation to this question.

Option 2: Explore "Anticipated Fruits" with reflection sheet. (25 minutes)

- *Set the context.* **According to our author, one way fruits become a touchstone for us in discernment is through anticipating possible outcomes to our choices. We are going to take time with a personal reflection sheet to help us imagine forward to anticipated fruits of a decision. Then we will share our insight in pairs, and our experience of the process in the whole group.**

- *Invite meditation with a reflection sheet* (encourage participants to spread around the room).

Share in pairs. (10 minutes)

Invite participants to share with a partner whatever they may be ready or willing to share. If any feel uncomfortable sharing the content of their reflections, they may choose to speak of what was helpful or difficult about the process.

Group debriefing (5 minutes)

Gather the group to share responses to the process (not personal content) of this reflection time. **What was it like to imagine forward, or project, anticipated fruits of our choices?**

CLOSING (10 MINUTES)

Sing a song of your choosing.

Read John 13:35. Allow a minute of silence.

Introduce the question of the week, written on a 3 by 5 card: "What choices have I made today that opened me to grow in the fruits of the Spirit, and what choices have I made that blocked such growth?" Invite group members to place their cards in a visible location (bathroom mirror, car dashboard, computer monitor) where they will see them several times a day.

Indicate that living with a question like this over the week will continue for a while longer. Encourage participants to spend three to five minutes a day reflecting on and journaling about the question, simply letting responses emerge and deepen. Responses will again be gathered during next week's Sharing Insights time.

Offer a closing prayer:

Teach us your ways, God of Wisdom,
for you are righteous and just.
Plant your Word in our hearts, water it
from the streams of your ever flowing mercy,
that it may bloom and produce in us
the fruit that is a blessing to you
and pleasing in your sight. Amen.[2]

Proclaim a brief blessing, such as "Go in peace."

Anticipated Fruits

Personal Reflection Sheet

1. Identify a question in your personal or work life that you currently struggle with—a decision or choice you don't have clarity about. (If you honestly can't identify such a question, select a significant decision you have previously struggled with, and put the questions under #3 below into past tense, imagining forward.)

2. Think of two to four possible paths forward. On the back of this reflection sheet, create a column for each path and name it at the top.

3. Read Galatians 5:16-26. Then project yourself imaginatively into the future.

   • Which of these "works of the flesh" are actual temptations in your life that could (or did) impact your choice of the path forward?

   • Which fruits of the Spirit are strongest in your life, and how might (or did) these influence your decision about a possible path forward?

   • How might each choice of path help or hinder cultivation of spiritual fruits you seek to grow in? Write your responses in each column.

   • What other fruits can you envision coming from each choice? Under the columns, write or draw a symbol of what you might anticipate.

4. Pray about what you perceive. Ask for increased clarity if needed, and listen for God's response.

Week 4

Core Identity as Touchstone

PREPARATION

Prepare yourself spiritually. If helpful, review your role as small-group leader in the Leader's Guide introduction. Read the article for Week 4, reflect on the daily exercises, and journal your responses. Pray for openness to the guidance of the Holy Spirit throughout this meeting. Pray also for participants to know more deeply their core identity in God's love, and to recognize their primary gifts—those that bring the most satisfaction, joy, and peace. Pray that group members will find freedom to claim and use their gifts as a touchstone in discerning God's will for their lives.

Prepare materials and the meeting space.

- Refer to Weekly Needs at a Glance (beginning on p. 23 of this guide). Review items listed under All Meetings and under Week 4.

- Consider your meeting space. Arrange chairs in a circle or around a table. Include a worship focus area with a cloth, Christ candle, and perhaps a symbol invoking the week's theme of identity in God's love (heart, cross, and bowl of water to represent baptism).

- Post the ground rules and Candle Prayer (if used) in a visible place.

- Make sufficient copies of the reflection sheet "Finding Freedom to Be Alive in God" (p. 66) for Deeper Explorations.

- Write the question of the week from the Closing on 3 by 5 cards for everyone.

- Review the Weekly Meeting so you can lead without simply reading from the book.

- Select songs or recorded music for the Opening and Closing.

Review the intent of this meeting: to continue practicing simple group discernment around a central question from the previous week, and to consider our core identity in God as a second touchstone for discerning God's will.

OPENING (10 MINUTES)

Welcome participants personally as they enter. Begin close to starting time to encourage punctuality. Welcome latecomers with a smile and gesture to find their seats.

Set the context.

This week we will pay attention to our core identity—who we really are; our unique gifts; what brings us gladness, energy, and peace. These are important touchstones for discernment. First, we'll share from the question we've pondered all week about choices we've made that either helped or blocked us in growing spiritual fruits. Then we will delve more deeply into what makes us come alive in God!

Join together in worship.

- Light the Christ candle, and recite the Candle Prayer or offer words like these: **Friends, remember the real presence of Christ, embracing us as one body with differently gifted members. We trust that exploring our uniquely created life and talents will help us discern faithful paths of expressing Christ's love in this world.**

- Read Psalm 139:13-18. Invite everyone to ponder how wonderfully God has knit each of us into unique individuals, and to consider God's purposes for our particular lives. Allow a few minutes of quiet (participants may wish to reread the text in their Bibles).

- Invite brief prayers from the group, closing with your own prayer.

- Sing "Loving Spirit" (URW #203) or a song of your choosing.

- Offer these closing words, from Irenaeus of Lyon (second century):

  It is not you who shape God,
  *   it is God who shapes you.*
  If, then, you are the work of God,
  *   await the hand of the artist who does all things in due season.*
  Offer the Potter your heart,
  *   soft and tractable,*
  *   and keep the form in which the Artist has fashioned you.*[1]

- Say or sing a blessing.

SHARING INSIGHTS (45 MINUTES)

During this time, participants will share how they have experienced God's presence this past week, drawing on experiences in response to the week's reading and daily exercises. Begin by considering the question from last week's Closing, as indicated below. If you find that most in the group have not spent time reflecting on this question, move ahead to the article and daily exercises.

- Ask group members to briefly review their journal entries in response to the week's article and daily exercises. Invite them also to review any reflections on the question of the week given at last meeting's Closing. *(5 minutes)*

- Encourage everyone to be attentive to God's presence in the group, and to what the Spirit may say through one another.

- Begin by guiding a brief reflection process *(10–15 minutes)* on last week's closing question, using these guidelines:

Invite quiet, holding in awareness the question we have lived with this past week: **What choices have I made today that opened me to grow in the fruit of the Spirit, and what choices have I made that blocked such growth?**

- Ask participants to share, as they are ready, just one choice that seemed especially important. Encourage prayerful listening to one another.

- After the sharing, return to quiet. Then invite any further perceptions that may have arisen as a result of hearing one another.

- Note aloud any common themes, and invite a moment of quiet gratitude.

- Continue with sharing from the week's reading and daily exercises. As leader, set the tone by offering your own response first, modeling brevity.

- In the last three to five minutes, invite all to reflect on this time and identify any common themes/patterns that might suggest a deeper message for the group.

- Note these in your journal so you can track themes/patterns through your weeks together and lift them up at appropriate moments.

BREAK (10 MINUTES)

DEEPER EXPLORATIONS (45 MINUTES)

Attending to our core identity

Set the context.

The author's math teacher stressed an ancient wisdom saying: "Know yourself." In our faith tradition, we cannot truly know ourselves apart from God, since we are made in the divine image. Knowing who God has created us to be in our uniqueness takes daily attention and spiritual awareness. To discern important decisions and changes in our lives, we need to know ourselves, to recognize the core identity and gifts God has given each one of us. Our Deeper Explorations exercise will help us pay closer attention to this uniqueness.

Introduce the personal reflection sheet "Finding Freedom to Be Alive in God." (20 minutes)

Ask participants to prayerfully ponder the questions, journaling their responses directly on the reflection sheet. They may wish to find a space apart in the room for this time.

Share in pairs. (10 minutes) [*If your group is well bonded, you may choose to dispense with the paired sharing and give more time to the plenary sharing.]

Invite participants to partner with one other person and share what they choose from their reflection time with these questions.

*Guide plenary sharing (*10 minutes)*

Draw the group back together and ask questions such as:

- Were there any surprises as you considered where you are most alive in God?
- What stands in the way of our becoming more alive to God? (Gather common themes.)
- What can free us to decide/move/act in the ways we feel beckoned?

Review the experience. (5 minutes)

Invite reflections on what we learn about ourselves from this whole exercise that might help us with future personal discernment.

CLOSING (10 MINUTES)

Sing or listen to a song of your choosing.

Read Romans 12:1-2. Allow a silent pause. Then ask, "Where is the Spirit calling you to live as a beloved child of God rather than as a child of the world's expectations?" Allow a minute or two of quiet.

Invite spoken prayers to emerge from your silent listening. Close with the Lord's Prayer.

Read Romans 12:2-5. Then hand out the question of the week, written on 3 by 5 cards: "Where do I sense that the church is being called to live from its beloved identity in God rather than from the world's expectations?" Invite participants once again to place their cards in a location where they will see it several times a day (you might ask them to share briefly what places they have found most effective).

Indicate that living with a question like this over the week will continue for a while longer. Encourage everyone to spend three to five minutes a day reflecting/journaling with the question. Responses will again be gathered during next week's Sharing Insights time.

Remind all of the date and time of your next meeting. Continue to encourage building daily spiritual practice through the reading and daily exercises. Offering a structure to develop the habit of daily spiritual reflection is one of the great gifts of *Companions in Christ.*

Offer a closing blessing. Suggestion: Galatians 13:13.

Finding Freedom to Be Alive in God
Personal Reflection Sheet

1. Where do you feel most alive in God? What feels like a place of real creativity, fulfillment, freedom, and joy?

2. What invites or urges you to greater growth in this experience of aliveness?

3. What stands in the way of your responding?

4. Reflect with your hand by drawing a picture to represent this challenge (use the back of this sheet). Allow your pen/pencil to depict what you long for, and what blocks you. Then let your imagination help you draw a way around or through the block. What might this path represent for you?

5. Where can you say no so you have more time/energy for this aliveness in God? Where can you say yes for the same purpose? (If you don't have time for this final question, take it home for further reflection.)

Week 5

Growing in the Gift

PREPARATION

Prepare yourself spiritually. Read the article for Week 5, reflect and journal with the daily exercises, and pray for the Holy Spirit's guidance during the upcoming meeting. Pray for your group to grow in its capacity to receive the gift of discernment, including deeper commitment to spiritual disciplines that open us to guidance, an ear for questions to live into, and greater willingness to perceive and follow God's yearning.

Prepare materials and meeting space.

- Refer to Weekly Needs at a Glance. Review items listed under All Meetings and under Week 5.

- Consider your meeting space, arranging chairs in circle or around table. Include a worship focus area with a cloth, Christ candle, and symbols invoking the week's theme of receptivity to the gift of discernment (empty bowl, picture of open hands).

- Post ground rules and Candle Prayer (if used) in visible place.

- List on newsprint or create a handout of the three "Preconditions for Discernment" found in Deeper Explorations.

- Make sufficient copies of the two handouts—"Gestation Model of Personal Discernment" (p. 74) and "Psalm 131" (p. 75)—for Deeper Explorations.

- Write the question of the week from the Closing on 3 by 5 cards for everyone.

- Review the Weekly Meeting so you can lead without simply reading from the book. Familiarize yourself especially with the group *lectio* process you will lead with Psalm 131 (see Leader's Note, p. 73).

- Select songs or recorded music for the Opening and Closing.

Review the intent of this meeting: to continue practicing group discernment around a central question from the previous week, to set this practice in a larger framework, and to claim the priority of cultivating a holy intention to desire God's desires through a willing spirit.

OPENING (10 MINUTES)

Welcome participants personally as they enter. Start on time, welcoming latecomers.

Set the context.

This is now our fifth week together, the midpoint of our adventure into the realm of discernment. Today we will put into a larger framework our weekly practice of listening together to a question, and spend some time exploring what it takes to cultivate the holy intention of wanting what God wants.

Join together in worship.

- Light the Christ candle, and offer the Candle Prayer or words like these: **Let us remember the risen, ascended Christ, who is still the Light of the world and so, by the grace of the Holy Spirit, is willing even now to guide our steps into the way and will of God.**

- Offer the group a brief context for the passage you are about to read: The prophet Samuel has been charged by God with anointing a new king over Israel after Saul's reign. Read 1 Samuel 16:4-7. Emphasize verse 7: "For the LORD does not see as mortals see; . . . but the LORD looks on the heart." Remind the group that discernment involves seeking God's way of seeing. Ask participants to ponder quietly situations or relationships in which they need to grow in God's way of seeing.

- Invite sentence prayers from the group, gathering them with your own words of prayer to close.

- Sing a song of your choosing.

- Offer these closing words from Dag Hammarskjöld:
  "Not I, but God in me."[1]
  You might suggest this as a breath prayer for the coming week.

- Say or sing a blessing.

SHARING INSIGHTS (45 MINUTES)

During this time, participants will share how they have experienced God's presence this past week, drawing on experiences in response to the week's reading and daily exercises. Begin by considering the question from last week's Closing, as indicated below.

- Ask group members to briefly review journal entries in response to the week's article and daily exercises, as well as reflections on the question of the week from last meeting's Closing. *(5 minutes)*

- Encourage deep attentiveness to God's presence in the group and to what the Spirit may say through one another.

- Begin by guiding a brief reflection process *(10–15 minutes)* on last week's closing question, using these guidelines:

Invite quiet, holding in awareness the question we have lived with this past week: **Where do I sense that the church is being called to live from its beloved identity in God rather than from the world's expectations?**

- Ask participants to share, as they are ready, just one instance of this call that felt especially striking or significant to them.

- After sharing, return to quiet. Invite further noticings that may have arisen as you have listened to one another. Is a Voice sounding through all your words?

- Note aloud any echoes or themes, and invite silent gratitude.

- Continue now sharing from the week's reading and daily exercises. As leader, set the tone by offering your own response first, modeling brevity.

- In the last three to five minutes, invite all to reflect back over this time and identify any common themes/patterns that might suggest a deeper message for the group.

- Note these so you can continue tracking themes and patterns through your weeks together, lifting them up at appropriate moments.

BREAK (10 MINUTES)

Deeper Explorations (45 minutes)

Cultivating holy indifference

Set the context. (1 minute)

Christians through the ages have wanted to do the will of God. The process of discovering what God wants and values for us is called discernment. One definition of discernment is "to see as God sees." We are going to spend some time now preparing to take up a receptive posture for listening to God's voice, sensing God's direction, and "seeing as God sees."

Introduce the personal discernment process of the Gestation Model. (5 minutes)

- Distribute the handout "Gestation Model of Personal Discernment."

- Indicate that this is a larger framework for a model we have been testing in abbreviated form for five weeks now—living with a question over time, pondering, praying, journaling, and sharing responses with others in the group.

- Point out that this is a helpful process for personal discernment, and a more natural, organic model than the carefully structured Ignatian method, for example.

- Then lift up the very first step: having a holy intention to want what God wants. Indicate that this step comes first in every way, and that we need to explore further what it means both spiritually and emotionally, since we can't go far into authentic discernment without building on this foundation.

Describe "Preconditions for Discernment." (5 minutes)

Point out the three preconditions you have listed on newsprint or handout:

1. "Holy relationship"—Have a living relationship with God

2. "Holy indifference"—Want God's will more than your own

3. "Holy obedience"—Commit to acting on what you discern as God's will

Expand briefly on the first point: **God is known and revealed to us in Jesus Christ, by the gracious power of the Holy Spirit. It is through the Spirit that we discern the mind of Christ and the will of God. Discernment comes to those who cultivate a living, receptive relationship with the divine Spirit.**

Explain *holy indifference* with words like these: "Holy indifference" does not mean we don't care about the outcome. It means we care enough about what God desires and intends that we are willing to lay aside our own desires, prejudices, or biases in the matter. As we let go of our own agendas, we open up an empty space inside that the Spirit can fill. Releasing our will allows us to listen to God in true openness and freedom. This is the willingness our author writes of in the week's reading.

Connect now to the *lectio* exercise: **But coming to holy indifference can be the hardest part of the discernment process. It means wanting God's will more than our own! So we're going to practice opening ourselves to willingness in a spirit of trust. It is difficult to act in holy obedience without feeling first a certain peace and acceptance of the divine will.**

Lead a group lectio *with Psalm 131. (25 minutes)*

[See Leader's Note on p. 73 to review the process of group *lectio*. Bold print may be spoken.]

- Give each participant a copy of the Psalm 131 handout.

- Explain the basic steps of *lectio* before leading it, including permission to pass on sharing at any stage, and how to pray for each other at the end.

- Guide group *lectio* according to the Leader's Note process.

Review the experience. (10 minutes)

Invite reflections on what we learn both from the practice and the psalm about cultivating willingness. You might ask specific questions such as:

- **Why is the image of the weaned child important?** (A weaned child is not grasping/striving for anything at the mother's breast but is simply content to rest.)

- **What does it say to you that this psalm is attributed to King David?** (Even those in highest positions of leadership/responsibility are like small children in relation to God, and need to learn to rest in trust—a hard posture for many leaders!)

- How might this psalm help us move toward holy indifference or deeper willingness to receive God's way?

Note aloud that **sometimes we can't achieve complete indifference before a discernment process. It is then important to acknowledge to ourselves and others that we still feel attached to a particular outcome, and to keep seeking greater interior freedom.**

CLOSING (10 MINUTES)

Sing a song of your choosing.

Read Romans 12:1. After a pause, invite participants to reflect on the spiritual worship of their living sacrifice to God. What do these phrases mean to them, and how do they connect? Allow a minute or so of silence.

Invite the group to reflect quietly on this question: **What might you need to give up or let go so that you can grow in your ability to discern God's will?**

Invite spoken prayers to emerge from the silence. Close with the Lord's Prayer.

Hand out the question of the week, written on 3 by 5 cards: "When am I most likely to become willful, and what most frees me from what I cling to tightly so that I become more open to God's leading?"

Remind participants to place their cards in a visible location. Encourage three to five minutes a day of reflection and journaling with the question. At the next meeting, responses will again be gathered during the Sharing Insights time.

Offer a closing blessing. Suggestion: Galatians 6:18.

Leader's Note
A PROCESS FOR GROUP *LECTIO*

Preparation: Take a moment to come fully into the present.... Sit comfortably alert, close your eyes, and center yourself with breathing....

1. Hear the word that is addressed personally to you.

As you hear this reading the first time, listen for the word or phrase that attracts you or catches your attention. Repeat it softly to yourself during the silence.

Read the text. After a minute, invite each person to say aloud only the word or phrase that caught their attention, without elaboration or response from anyone.

2. Ask, "How is my life touched by this word?"

As you hear it a second time, listen for how this psalm touches your life today. Consider possibilities and be open to sensory impressions during the silence.

After two minutes, invite participants to speak a sentence or two about how the text touches them, perhaps beginning with the words, *I hear, I see, I sense, I feel.* (Or pass.)

3. Ask, "Is there an invitation here for me?"

In this third reading, listen for a possible invitation that is relevant to you in the next few days. Ponder your sense of divine invitation in the silence.

After several minutes, invite the group to speak their sense of invitation (or pass). Ask them to pay special attention to the invitation expressed by the person on their right.

4. Pray for one another's empowerment to respond.

We are going to pray now, aloud or silently, for God to help the person on your right respond to the sense of invitation expressed. (As leader, begin, followed by the person on your left. Move around the circle to the left as you pray for the person on the right, so the person receiving prayer is freed from thinking how to pray for the next person. If the person on your right passed at step 3, pray silently and squeeze the hand of the person on your left to signal when you have finished praying.)

Group members may share their feelings about the process after completing these steps.

Adapted from *Gathered in the Word: Praying the Scripture in Small Groups* by Norvene Vest (Nashville: Upper Room Books, 1996), 27. Used by permission.

Gestation Model of Personal Discernment

- Have a holy intention of wanting what God wants in this situation.

- Let the question for discernment rise up from your depths, planted in you by God.

- Live with the question: work with it, rest with it, talk about it with others you trust, read with the question in mind.

- Continue listening in every way you can: in circumstances, small signs, the words of others, scripture, nature, dreams, inner promptings, the language of your body.

- Be alert to movement of any kind: a change in the shape of the question, inner or outer nudges, feelings of new energy or of being drained, growing clarity.

- Patiently await for emergence of the answer to your question. It will come to birth in God's own time, and you will recognize it when it emerges fully into the light of day.

Adapted from material developed by Susan W. N. Ruach. Used with permission.

Psalm 131

Yahweh, my heart has no lofty ambitions,

my eyes do not look too high.

I am not concerned with great affairs

or marvels beyond my scope.

Enough for me to keep my soul tranquil and quiet

like a child in its mother's arms,

as content as a child that has been weaned.

Israel, rely on Yahweh,

now and for always!

Week 6

In the Hard Places

PREPARATION

Prepare yourself spiritually. Read the article for Week 6, reflect and journal with the daily exercises, and pray to be guided by the Holy Spirit during the upcoming meeting. Pray for your group to grow: (1) in their ability to discern the gifts of waiting, and (2) in awareness of daily experiences of consolation and desolation.

Prepare your materials and meeting space.

- Refer to Weekly Needs at a Glance. Review items listed under All Meetings and Week 6.

- Consider your meeting space, arranging chairs in a circle or around a table. Include a worship focus area with a cloth, Christ candle, and symbols invoking the week's theme of waiting, desolation, and consolation ("Stop" sign, empty bowl, and full bowl).

- Post ground rules and Candle Prayer (if used) in a visible place.

- Have newsprint available to write responses on during Deeper Explorations.

- Have crayons/colored pencils available for Deeper Explorations.

- Write the question of the week from Closing on 3 by 5 cards for everyone.

- Review the Weekly Meeting so you can lead without simply reading from the book. Decide whether to engage in question-of-the-week process or to give the whole Sharing Insights time to reflections around daily exercises.

- Select songs/recorded music for Opening and Closing.

Review the intent of this meeting: to share experiences of waiting on God, and to explore the sense of both consolation and desolation in our lives with particular emphasis on consolations and the importance of remembering/savoring these graces.

OPENING (10 MINUTES)

Welcome participants personally as they enter.

Set the context.

In this, our sixth meeting, we will (continue listening to a question together and then) share perspectives on waiting for God. We will also spend time recognizing and naming our experiences of consolation and desolation, focusing especially on consolation and its sustaining grace in hard times. [Adapt this wording according to your choice about how to use group time.]

Light the Christ candle and recite the Candle Prayer or offer words like these:
This light represents the risen Lord Christ, who fills our hearts with gifts of sustaining grace in all circumstances, and who continues to provide light for our path in life.

Read 1 Thessalonians 5:16-24. After a moment of quiet, read it again. Ask, **What encouragement and hope do you hear in this passage?** Allow more silence.

Invite group members to pray with eyes open, naming in a phrase or sentence the hope and encouragement each one hears in this Word. Invite the group to respond with a phrase like *Dear God, thank you!* after each person's words. Close by gathering up the group's gratitude to God in your own words.

Sing a song. Suggestion: "Spirit of God, Descend upon My Heart" (UMH #500; include stanza 4, which includes these words: "Teach me the struggles of the soul to bear . . . ").

Offer a blessing, using 1 Thessalonians 5:28.

SHARING INSIGHTS (45 MINUTES)

During this time, participants will share how they have experienced God's presence this past week, drawing on experiences in response to the week's reading and daily exercises. If you believe your group would benefit from more time to share responses to the daily exercises, you may choose to omit the question-of-the-week reflection process.

- Ask group members to briefly review their journal entries in response to the week's article and daily exercises (as well as reflections on the question of the week from last meeting's Closing). *(5 minutes)* [Adapt instructions as necessary.]

- Encourage deep attentiveness to God's presence in the group, and to what the Spirit may say through one another.

- Begin by guiding a brief reflection process *(10-15 minutes)* on last week's closing question, using the following guidelines. [*This step is optional.*]

Invite quiet, holding in awareness the questions we have lived with this past week: **When am I most likely to become willful? What most frees me from what I cling to tightly so that I become more open to God's leading?**

- Ask participants to share, as they are ready, just one area each felt especially called to let go in order to more freely discern God's way.

- After sharing, return to quiet. Invite further noticings that may have arisen as you have listened to one another. Is a Voice sounding through your words?

- Note aloud any echoes or themes, and invite silent gratitude.

- Continue with sharing from the week's reading and daily exercises, with special emphasis given to Exercises 1 and 4. As leader, model honesty and brevity by first offering your own response to one of these exercises.

- In the last three to five minutes, invite all to reflect back over this time and identify any common themes/patterns that might suggest a deeper message for the group.

- Note these so you can continue tracking themes and patterns through your weeks together, lifting them up at appropriate moments.

BREAK (10 MINUTES)

DEEPER EXPLORATIONS (45 MINUTES)

Identifying core experiences of consolation and desolation

Set the context.

In order to grow in discernment, we need to learn to recognize the most basic movements in our spirit on a daily basis. This first exercise in our Deeper Explorations will help us begin to recognize the essential experience of consolation and desolation in our personal lives.

Guide reflection on experiences of centeredness and off-centeredness. (25 minutes)

- **Get in touch with a core spiritual experience in your life when you felt deeply centered in or surrounded by grace. If several experiences come to mind, choose one.** (Allow a minute for people to consider and choose a remembrance.)

- **What does it feel like physically and emotionally to stay with this experience in your memory? Describe your feelings in words or colors or images.** [Participants may use crayons/colored pencils with their journals in a spontaneous, sketchy way.] *(2 minutes)*

- Share around your group the words/colors/images that surface for each person. List key words on newsprint. Where do you find common ground in these experiences of grace? What differences do you discover? How are these commonalities and differences illuminating or challenging? Name key insights. *(10 minutes)*

- **Now get in touch with a core experience of an obstacle, a difficulty, or a frustration in your life, in which you felt off-center or ungrounded spiritually. If several instances come to mind, choose just one.** (Allow another minute.)

- **Describe in words, colors, or images what this experience is like, both physically and emotionally.** *(2 minutes)*

- Share again around the group, noting commonalities and differences and what you learn from them. *(10 minutes)*

- Point out that this exercise can help us begin to pay attention to the basic movements of discernment. In learning to recognize consolation and desolation, where we feel in sync or out of sync with God in daily life, we lay the foundation for recognizing these same movements in a group or community.

Guide a further exploration of consolation. (20 minutes)

- Indicate that this is an opportunity to look deeper into our experiences of consolation—times of special blessing in our lives we often take for granted. We will consider how to savor them so they can strengthen us in the hard times.

- Invite people to reflect over the past month and ask themselves: *What particular consolations—special blessings and graces from God—have I experienced in this time?* Give the group three minutes to reflect and jot responses in their journals.

- Next, invite participants to ask themselves: *How have I savored these blessings, or how can I savor them more fully?* Allow two minutes for reflection/journaling.

- Have group members form triads to share responses to the questions and listen deeply to one another. *(10 minutes)* [If you are running short of time, form pairs.]

- Gather everyone and ask, **What has our sharing helped us see about the abundance of God's consolations, or about ways we can savor them when they come?** *(5 minutes)*

CLOSING (10 MINUTES)

Sing or listen to a song of your choosing.

Invite a time of quiet thankfulness for any insights that have come in the consideration of God's consolations. [Or you may choose to make this a time for spoken prayers in place of the spoken prayers below.]

Read Psalm 51:10–12. Guide a simple examen with the following questions. Invite the group to reflect quietly after each question and jot what they notice in their journals:

- **When did I feel new energy or joy in this meeting time? How do I notice this in my body?**

- **When did I feel drained, anxious, or tired in this meeting? How do I notice this in my body?**

- **When was I most aware of God's presence? How do I notice this in my spirit?**

- **When was I least aware of God's presence? How do I notice this in my spirit?**

Invite spoken prayers, ending with the Lord's Prayer.

Hand out the questions of the week, written on 3 by 5 cards: "What consolations are coming to me this week? How am I savoring them or allowing them to sustain me in desolation?"

Remind participants to place their card in a visible location and spend a few minutes each day reflecting on the questions and journaling about them. Responses may be gathered during the Sharing Insights time next week.

Offer a closing blessing, using 2 Thessalonians 3:16.

Week 7
Communal Discernment—Beginnings

PREPARATION

Prepare yourself spiritually. Read the article for Week 7, reflect and journal with the daily exercises, and pray to be fully open to the Holy Spirit as you make choices concerning the group meeting and during the meeting itself. Pray that participants will perceive more clearly how they have already engaged in communal discernment during these seven weeks, and that they will be ready to grow further in corporate practices of discerning divine guidance.

Prepare your materials and meeting space.

- Refer to Weekly Needs at a Glance and review items listed for Week 7.

- Arrange your meeting space with chairs in a circle (not around a table) for the Clearness Committee process. Prepare the worship focus area with a cloth, Christ candle, and perhaps a symbol of listening, such as a conch shell.

- Review the Weekly Meeting so familiarity can free you from overdependence on the written words printed in this Leader's Guide.

- The Clearness Committee process in Deeper Explorations will require advance preparation for the focus person, and the role of clerk needs to be well understood to establish the right climate and help the group formulate appropriate questions.

- Decide to prepare yourself either for the role of clerk or focus person in the Clearness Committee. If you have a coleader, decide between you which roles to take. If you have no coleader and choose to be the focus person, select a group member you can brief on the role of clerk. If you choose to be clerk, invite the group member in advance to prepare to be the focus person. Use the handout "Clearness Committee Description" to help interpret both roles.

- Whoever prepares for the role of focus person should choose a real issue she or he hopes to find clarity on and that can be shared willingly with the group. A brief statement (1–2 paragraphs) about the issue/options being considered should be written up before meeting, and copies made for everyone.

- Make copies for everyone of two handouts: "Clearness Committee Description" (pp. 89–90) and "Sample Questions for a Clearness Committee" (p. 91).

- If you use it, post the Candle Prayer in a visible place.

- Write the question of the week from the Closing on 3 by 5 cards for everyone.

- Select songs/recorded music for the Opening and Closing.

Note: This is one Weekly Meeting where it could be especially beneficial to break the content into two separate meetings. You could then give plenty of time one week to Sharing Insights (for both the question of the week and daily exercises), and also introduce the Clearness Committee process (using both handouts) to help prepare members for the next week. The following week, you could give full attention to the Clearness Committee experience, which will always benefit from additional time. This option could also allow meetings to be shortened somewhat (1½ hours).

Review the intent of this meeting: to experience an abbreviated Clearness Committee as a fruitful way to engage a group in aiding the discernment of an individual.

OPENING (10 MINUTES)

Welcome participants personally as they enter.

Set the context.

This is our seventh meeting. Have you noticed that (almost) every time we meet, we have engaged in some form of communal as well as personal discernment? For example, we have frequently shared what we are discerning together in relation to a particular question—the question of the week. Today we will expand our repertoire of group discernment practices with the Clearness Committee described in this week's article. (Adapt words as needed.)

Light the Christ candle, and recite the Candle Prayer or offer words like these:

This light represents the radiance of Christ, who fills our hearts with sustaining grace and provides light for our journeys. We intentionally place God at the center of our meeting with this symbol of Holy Presence.

Read Luke 17:20-21 and Matthew 13:44-45. Make a connection to this effect: **Jesus says that the kingdom of God is within and among us and that the kingdom of heaven is like a pearl buried in a field, of greater value than anything else. Perhaps Jesus is telling us that the reign of God, the "kingdom pearl," is buried within us, personally and collectively.**

Let me invite you to take a few moments to let go of lesser concerns and focus your attention on the kingdom pearl buried within your own soul. . . . How might you uncover this most precious gift? Imagine what layers you need to excavate in order to discover, or recover, the reign of God deep in your being. . . . (Pause a sufficient time for reflection.) And can you find an image now for the kingdom pearl buried among us—in our small group or congregation? . . . How might we recover this gift? . . .

Invite prayers from the group, closing with your own brief words.

Sing or listen to a song/hymn. Suggestion: a sung version of the Lord's Prayer.

Offer a blessing.

SHARING INSIGHTS (45 MINUTES)

During this time, participants will share how they have experienced God's presence this past week, drawing on experiences in response to the week's reading and daily exercises. If you believe your group would benefit from more time to share responses to the daily exercises, you may choose to omit the question-of-the-week reflection process.

- Ask group members to briefly review journal entries in response to the week's article and daily exercises (as well as reflections on the question of the week from last meeting's Closing). *(5 minutes)* [Adapt instructions as necessary.]

- Encourage deep attentiveness to God's presence in the group and to what the Spirit may say through one another.

- Begin by guiding a brief reflection process *(10–15 minutes)* on last week's closing question, using the following guidelines [at your discretion]:

Invite quiet, holding in awareness the questions we have lived with this past week: **What consolations are coming to me this week? How am I savoring them, or allowing them to sustain me in desolation?**

- Ask members to share, as they are ready, just one consolation from the week and how they have found joy or sustenance from it.

- After sharing, return to quiet. Invite further insights that may have arisen as a result of listening to one another. Is a Voice sounding beneath our words?

- Offer thanks to all who have shared and bless God for new understanding.

- Continue with sharing from the week's reading and daily exercises, giving special emphasis to Exercises 1 and 5. You may wish to begin this time by sharing from your own experience, or you may feel the group is ready to start without your taking the lead.

- As you share together around the last part of Exercise 5, you may experience the gift of collective discernment emerging. If so, name it as such, and indicate that discerning in community is itself an experience of the divine reign breaking in!

- In the last few minutes, invite all to think back and notice any patterns emerging from this time of shared reflection. If patterns can be identified, ask what they might suggest.

- Note patterns and themes so you can remind the group as appropriate.

BREAK (10 MINUTES)

DEEPER EXPLORATIONS (45 MINUTES)

Experiencing an abbreviated Clearness Committee

Set the context.

The Clearness Committee is a way for a trusted group of faithful friends to help an individual discern an important decision or direction in life. This process comes to us from the Quaker Christian tradition. We can't experience the entire process here, but we can get a fair taste of what this practice is like and how it works.

Review the Clearness Committee process. (10 minutes)

- Ask participants to read the handout "Clearness Committee Description." Respond to questions of clarification and reinforce important points verbally, such as that the purpose is not to be good problem solvers but to support the focus person in listening to his/her inner teacher (the Holy Spirit or indwelling Christ).

- Review the handout "Sample Questions for a Clearness Committee." Help your group grasp basic principles of open-ended questions that aid the focus person's discernment. Emphasize that the questioner cannot know the answer to such a question in advance.

Enter the Clearness Committee experience. (25 minutes)

- Identify the clerk and focus person for the group.

- Engage in the Clearness Committee process as described on the handout, as far as you can within your time frame. The clerk will need to reserve the last five minutes to invite the focus person to share what was most helpful (or unhelpful, as this is a learning process for the group).

- The clerk thanks members for their participation and invites further prayer support for the focus person in his/her continuing discernment. (If the focus person wishes to continue the process beyond this meeting, he or she needs to negotiate a time with the group.)

Reflect on the experience. (10 minutes)

- **What was this process like as a committee member?**

- **What was it like as the focus person?**

- **What potential can we see in this practice, and in what settings?**

Closing (10 minutes)

Sing or listen to a song of your choosing.

Read Psalm 51:6. Guide a simple examen with the following questions. Invite group members to reflect quietly after each question and jot what they notice in their journals:

- **Where did I feel new energy or joy in this meeting time?**

- **Where did I feel drained, anxious, or tired in this meeting?**

Ask if anyone has recognized the connection between this practice of examen and our experience with consolation and desolation. Point out how the examen offers us a simple way to discern the movements of God's Spirit in our daily experience.

Invite spoken prayers, ending with a brief prayer of thanksgiving.

Hand out the question of the week, written on 3 by 5 cards: "Where do I see the reign of Christ breaking into my experience?"

Remind participants to place their cards in a visible location and spend a few minutes each day reflecting on the question and journaling about it. Responses may be gathered during the Sharing Insights time next week.

Offer a closing blessing, using Ephesians 6:23.

Clearness Committee Description

The Clearness Committee is a structure for dealing with our dilemmas in the company of a few friends who can help us seek God's direction. Historically, Quakers used the Clearness Committee when two members of a local meeting (congregation) asked to be married. In the last century, Quakers expanded the approach to help individuals make a variety of important decisions.

Behind the Clearness Committee is a simple but crucial spiritual conviction: Each of us has an inner, divine light that gives us the guidance we need but is often obscured by various forms of inner and outer interference. The function of the Clearness Committee is not to give advice or "fix" people but to help them remove obstacles and discover the divine assistance that is within. Rooted in that conviction, the Clearness Committee can help people discover their own God-given leadings and callings through silence, questioning, listening, and prayer.

1. Generally, the person seeking clearness (focus person) writes down his or her situation before the meeting and circulates the statement to committee members. The issue should be identified as precisely as possible. This is the focus person's first step toward clearness. [Under certain conditions, this step can be accomplished through a clear statement at the first meeting.]

2. The focus person chooses his or her committee—five or six trusted individuals with as much diversity among them as possible. The committee should meet with the understanding that there may be a second and even a third meeting in subsequent weeks.

3. A clerk (facilitator) is named to open the meeting, close it, and serve as traffic cop, making sure the rules are followed and that everyone who wants to speak can do so.

4. Typically, the meeting begins with a period of centering silence. The focus person begins with a fresh summary of the issue. Then committee members speak, governed by a simple but demanding rule: Members must limit themselves to asking the focus person questions—honest, caring questions. This means no advice giving ("Why don't you . . . ?" or "My uncle had the same problem and he . . .") but only authentic, challenging, open, loving questions. Members guard against questions that arise from curiosity rather than care for the person's clarity about his or her inner truth. Such a question will be one the questioner could not possibly know the answer to. The clerk gently but firmly dismisses questions that are advice or judgment in disguise ("I believe this question does not meet the criteria we have agreed to").

5. Committee members should try to ask questions briefly and to the point. The focus person usually responds to questions as they are asked, keeping responses relatively brief. It is always the focus person's right, however, not to answer in order to protect privacy.

6. The pacing of the questioning and answering should be relaxed, gentle, and kind. Do not be afraid of silence in the group.

7. The Clearness Committee works best when everyone approaches it in a prayerful way, inwardly affirming the reality of each person's inner guidance and truth. We must give up the pretense that we can know another's truth or that we are obliged to save each other. Rather, we help one another pay attention to God's saving and guiding presence.

The Clearness Committee is a powerful way to rally the strength of community around a struggling soul, drawing deeply on that of God within each of us. The Clearness Committee has its dangers. But once the spiritual discipline is understood and embraced, it becomes a new channel for the spirit of God to move with grace and power in our midst.

Adapted from "The Clearness Committee: A Communal Approach to Discernment" by Parker J. Palmer, in *Communion, Community, Commonweal: Readings for Spiritual Leadership* (Nashville: Upper Room Books, 1995), 131–36. Used by permission of Upper Room Books.

Sample Questions for a Clearness Committee

- What possible outcomes do you foresee in each possibility you are considering?

- What are your best hopes in regard to this issue?

- What are your fears in regard to this issue? (Six months from now, what do you fear?)

- What do you sense God is saying to you about your hopes and fears?

- Where does God's deeper call in your life seem to be surfacing?

- What is your prayer like around this matter?

- When you think of this path, what color comes to mind? . . . What associations do you have with this color?

- What happens in your gut when you think about this possibility?

- What motivates you in considering this option?

- What criteria or values are most important to you as you consider this decision?

- Where do you feel joy, gladness, or energy in this matter?

- Where do you feel heaviness, sadness, or draining of energy?

- What need or desire would this direction fill for you? for others?

- What would be most life-giving for you in this situation?

- What would need to die in you for new life and freedom to come forth?

- What scripture passage or song comes to mind as you ponder this matter?

- Does anything in your previous experience of God's grace illuminate this issue?

These are simply examples of open-ended questions with no agenda behind them. They are asked to help with the focus person's own discernment process. Such questions have no right or wrong answer. Their only purpose is to help another person listen to his/her inner teacher (the Holy Spirit or the indwelling Christ).

Week 8
Communal Discernment—
Going Farther

PREPARATION

Prepare yourself spiritually. Read the article for Week 8 and reflect/journal with the daily exercises. Continue praying to be open to the Spirit's promptings during the group meeting so you can change course or bring to bear resources of your own spirit in relation to the process of the moment. Pray that God will enrich each participant's depth of understanding and Christlike character through their daily spiritual exercises, and that the group will grasp more fully both the nature of communal discernment and the variety of patterns that can be used to help elicit this gift.

Prepare materials and meeting space.

- Check Weekly Needs at a Glance to review items particular to Week 8.

- Arranging chairs in a circle will work best for the Deeper Explorations process. Your worship focus area this week might include a symbol of prayer in addition to the cloth and Christ candle.

- If you are using it, post the Candle Prayer in a visible place.

- Review the Weekly Meeting, especially Deeper Explorations, so you can lead comfortably without relying heavily on the text.

- Make enough copies of "Discerning God's Prayer in Us for Another" handout.

- Write the question of week from the Closing on 3 by 5 cards for everyone.

- Select songs/recorded music for the Opening and Closing.

Review the intent of this meeting: to continue sharing insights from personal daily reflection, and to experience a second group discernment process for the sake of one member that could be an alternative or complement to the Clearness Committee.

OPENING (10 MINUTES)

Welcome participants personally as they enter.

Set the context.

In this, our eighth meeting, we take another step together into communal discernment. We will further expand our tool kit of practices by experiencing another group discernment process for the sake of one person that can be a helpful alternative to the Clearness Committee we experienced last week.

Our group process this week does not correspond precisely with the article's focus on group discernment for faith communities. A looser relationship between the article and our Deeper Explorations will continue in these final few weeks, partly due to the nature of a small group like ours meeting for a limited time period. However, everything we are learning in these weeks together feeds our ability to move toward practices of discernment for the wider church—at the congregational level, and potentially at the level of larger ecclesial structures.

Light the Christ candle and offer words like these:

As we gather, let us remember the presence of Christ our Light among us. And may we open our hearts now to the mind and heart and spirit of Christ in our midst.

Read Philippians 2:1–5 (end with "Let the same mind be in you that was in Christ Jesus").

- After a pause, slowly reread verse 2.

- Ask everyone to ponder for a few minutes what it means to "have the mind of Christ" in us, and how this relates to our being "of the same mind, having the same love, being in full accord" as a community of his followers.

- Invite participants to share their insights in a few sentences. [If this seems especially rich for your group, give more time to it and adjust time elsewhere.]

- Gather up these insights in a prayer of thanks. Incorporate the idea that in all our efforts at discernment, personal or communal, we seek the mind of Christ.

Sing or listen to a song/hymn. Suggestions:
  "Christ Beside Me" (TFWS #2166)
  "More Like You" (TFWS #2167)

Offer a blessing.

SHARING INSIGHTS (45 MINUTES)

During this time, participants will share how they have experienced God's presence this past week, drawing on experiences in response to the week's reading and daily exercises. If you believe your group would benefit from more time to share responses to the daily exercises, you may omit the question-of-the-week reflection process.

- Ask group members to briefly review journal entries in response to the week's article and daily exercises (as well as reflections on the question of the week from last meeting's Closing). *(5 minutes)* [Adapt instructions as necessary.]

- Encourage deep attentiveness to God's presence in the group, and to what the Spirit may say through one another.

- Begin by guiding a brief reflection process *(10–15 minutes)* on last week's closing question, using the following guidelines [at your discretion]:

Invite quiet, holding in awareness the question we have lived with this past week: **Where do I see the reign of Christ breaking into my experience?**

- Ask members to share just one place/way they have sensed the reign of Christ breaking into their week.

- After all have shared, return to quiet. Then invite any insights that may have arisen as a result of listening to one another's sharing.

- Offer thanks to all who have shared, and bless God for new understanding.

- Continue with sharing from the week's reading and daily exercises, inviting perspectives/insights that were particularly meaningful. You may wish to begin this time by sharing from your own experience, or you may allow the group to start without your taking the lead.

- In the last few minutes, review this time together and notice if any themes or patterns emerge from the shared reflections. If so, ask if these suggest any prompting of the Spirit for the group as a whole. Give thanks.

BREAK (10 MINUTES)

DEEPER EXPLORATIONS (45 MINUTES)

Experiencing a model of group discernment for the sake of an individual

Set the context.

Last week we had a taste of the Clearness Committee, a process of communal aid in the discernment an individual. This week we have an opportunity to try another model that invites group discernment on behalf of one member. This process is adapted from one developed and used by the Shalem Institute.[1]

Perhaps two of you can experience being the discerner in the time we have available. Or we may choose to give more relaxed time to one discerner. And we always have the option of scheduling an extra meeting to make this opportunity available to others in the group.

Review the process using the handout "Discerning God's Prayer in Us for Another." *(5 minutes)*

- Give everyone a few minutes to read the handout, and respond to any questions of clarification about the process.

- Ask the group whether they would prefer to allow two members to experience being discerners and adhere to the time frames indicated on the handout, or to give more relaxed time to one discerner.

Guide the process. (35 minutes) [Adapt time frames below depending on group decision.]

- Ask for a volunteer in your group to be the first discerner.

- Invite the group into silence for three minutes. Remind them that during this time, the group prays for the discerner while the discerner asks God the questions suggested on the handout.

- After three minutes, invite the discerner to begin sharing what happened to him/her during the silence. Give a gentle reminder of the five-minute time frame. Remind others to simply listen without interrupting or giving advice, although questions of clarification are permitted.

- Invite silence for another three minutes, with a brief reminder that the discerner is now in open, receptive prayer, while group members hold in mind this question: *What is God's prayer in me for you?* ("you" being the discerner).

- After three minutes, invite responses to the discerner from what others have heard in the silence. Responses can be surprisingly different from what you might expect. If advice giving begins to creep in, gently guide responders back to the simple prayers they hear within for the discerner. Allow five to seven minutes for this feedback.

- Invite one more volunteer to be the discerner and repeat the pattern. If others in your group express the desire to experience being the discerner, you may want to schedule another meeting devoted entirely to continuing this process so everyone who wishes to can receive the gift of this way of prayer.

Take time to debrief the process. (5 minutes)

- **What has been valuable about this experience?**

- **What has been most surprising?**

- **Where or how might we benefit from this process in our common life?**

Note: You may feel led to interject verbal prayer for the discerner at some point in the process/debriefing, especially if strong feelings surface. Or there might be a meaningful song, poem, or blessing the group would like to offer the discerner. Stay open to what comes as a prompting of the Spirit, either within you or from the group.

CLOSING (10 MINUTES)

Sing or listen to a song of your choosing.

Read John 15:11. Guide a simple examen with the following questions. Invite the group to reflect quietly after each question and jot what they notice in their journals:

- **Where did I sense the greatest joy or energy in our group during this meeting?**

- **Where did I sense energy loss, boredom, or anxiety in the group?**

- **Do I notice any patterns in how or when God shows up for our group?**

Invite members to share reflections about where they sensed energy and joy as a group. Gather up the sense of grace with a spoken prayer of gratitude.

Hand out the question of the week, written on 3 by 5 cards: "What question might we adopt as a traveling companion over the next six months in relation to our congregation or faith community?"*

Urge participants to spend a few minutes each day reflecting and journaling about the question, since next week the sharing of responses to this question will serve an important purpose. Responses will be gathered during the Sharing Insights time and may also continue into the Closing.

*Sharing around this question will be important at the next meeting, so *please do not skip this step.* This reflection could result in a question group members carry with them well beyond the time frame of *The Way of Discernment* experience. Group members may feel they are not equipped to answer a question related to the larger faith community, or that it would be presumptuous to imagine a question on behalf of a whole congregation. Remind them that all of us are important to the life of the church and have perspectives to bring to those in leadership. They are neither seeking the ultimate question nor trying to usurp the role of church leaders, but simply seeking your group's contribution to the whole—what you may be called to continue discerning in relation to your wider faith community. If some in your group are from different churches, it may still be possible to discern a helpful common question to hold and pray with over time. If participants wonder about the value of such a question, suggest that there's no telling how God might use our continuing discernment for the body of Christ.

Offer a closing blessing: "Grace be with all of you" (Titus 3:15b).

Discerning God's Prayer in Us for Another

- One person in the group volunteers to be the first discerner.

- Begin with three minutes of silence. During this time, the group prays with open hearts for the discerner, and the discerner asks God questions such as:

  How have you been present in my life recently?
  What have you been telling me or trying to teach me about you? about myself?
  What is your prayer for me now?

- After three minutes, the discerner begins to share what happened to him/her during the silence. She or he may speak for up to five minutes. Others in the group simply listen without interrupting or giving advice. Questions of clarification are allowed.

- The group enters silence for another three minutes. During this time the discerner remains in receptive prayer while members of the group hold in mind the following question for the discerner: *What is God's prayer in me for you?*

- After three minutes, group members begin to share what they have heard in the silence with the discerner. Again, the rule is no advice giving; just focus on the prayer they hear in themselves for the discerner.

- After five to seven minutes for this feedback, one more group member may volunteer to be the discerner, and the pattern is repeated.

- The group leader will serve as timekeeper and reminder of the group process.

Based on a group spiritual direction process developed by Rose Mary Dougherty of Shalem Institute and adapted by Nora Gallagher. Used by permission.

Week 9
Elements of Perpetual Challenge

PREPARATION

Prepare yourself spiritually. Read the article for Week 9, and reflect/journal with the daily exercises. Pray to be available to the Spirit's guidance as you prepare for the group meeting, and to be open to God's promptings during the meeting so you can move nimbly with the dynamics of the group under the Spirit's leading. Ask God to grow the life of Christ in each participant through the daily spiritual exercises, and to help the group continue broadening and deepening their experience of communal discernment.

Prepare materials and the meeting space.

- Check Weekly Needs at a Glance to review items particular to Week 9.

- Again, arrange chairs in a circle for the Deeper Explorations. The worship focus area could include a cross, in addition to a cloth and Christ candle.

- Review the Weekly Meeting, especially Deeper Explorations so you can lead it comfortably. The three segments of Deeper Explorations move from personal reflection to the larger world, then back to the intermediary between person and world—the church. Reflecting first on how God's call to a holy life is expressed and what God yearns for in our world, we come back to how the Spirit may be inviting us to help reshape church life in relation to the world God loves. (You may need to help your group understand this as a valid subject for any congregational small group to explore, even if few or none of its members currently hold leadership roles. Remind them that the relationship of this small group to the wider faith community is of vital concern. Your purpose is not merely to enrich individuals but to help the church move toward deeper spiritual practice and discernment.)

- Preprint on newsprint or chalkboard the three headings for each column indicated under "Guide a reflection process" in Deeper Explorations.

- Review the Leader's Note for Deeper Explorations, adding your own ideas.

- Collect 3 by 5 cards for each participant for the Closing, in case the group identifies a long-term question beyond the time frame of this group.

- Select songs/recorded music for Opening and Closing.

Review the intent of this meeting: to continue sharing insights from personal daily reflection, and to experience a group prayer process focused on the wider community that might also help the group discern a common calling within the church.

OPENING (10 MINUTES)

Welcome participants personally as they enter.

Set the context.

This is our ninth and next-to-last meeting. We will be building on the practice of communal discernment we tried out last week. But instead of asking what God's prayer is for us personally, we will be seeking God's yearning for the larger community of church and world, and how we hear that prayer in our minds and hearts. The prophetic call of Micah will be our guide.

Light the Christ candle and offer words like these:

As we gather, may the light of Christ shine on our path and direct us in the way that leads to life—life not only for us in this group, but also for the church and the world God loves so much.

Read Micah 6:8. Remind group that in Daily Exercise 2 we had time to reflect on this text personally. Now we want to reflect on how it speaks to us together.

Invite silent reflection on these questions:

What might the Lord require of us not just individually but as a small group? Is there a larger purpose in God calling us together at this time? (Allow a few minutes of silence.)

Invite responses, letting them slowly surface.

Ask participants to articulate common themes they might hear.

Offer a brief prayer of thanks for any coalescing sense of direction or stirring of possibility.

Sing a song as a blessing. Suggestion: "They'll Know We Are Christians by Our Love" (TFWS #2223)

SHARING INSIGHTS (45 MINUTES)

During this time, participants share how they have experienced God's presence this past week, starting with reflections on the question of the week, then drawing on experiences in response to the week's reading and daily exercises. It is important to reflect on the question of the week this time, rather than making it optional.

• Allow a minute for all to review personal journal reflections on the question of the week from last meeting's Closing. Then guide a brief sharing time, using the process indicated below. *(10-15 minutes)*

Invite quiet, holding in awareness the question we have lived with this past week: **What question might we adopt as a traveling companion over the next six months in relation to our congregation or faith community?**

• Ask members to share any question that has come to them persistently, energetically, or even tentatively this past week.

• After all have shared, invite a minute or two of quiet to listen for anything that might be surfacing in or through all the possibilities.

• Then invite members to consider whether/where they perceive a common-ground question or can state a new question encompassing several others. (Remember, you are neither seeking the ultimate question nor trying to usurp the role of church leaders; you are simply seeking your contribution to the whole—what your group is called to continue discerning in relation to your wider faith community.)

• See if you can come to consensus on a question that seems sufficiently broad and helpful for all to accept. As leader, contribute any suggestions that seem appropriate. (If there is a significant question to carry, it should surface fairly readily. If no authentic question comes to the fore, don't belabor this process. Simply let it go.)

• If you find a good long-term question, capture it in writing. Tell your members they'll have a chance to write it on a 3 by 5 card at the Closing.

- Now give participants a few minutes to review briefly their journal entries in response to the week's article and daily exercises.

- Invite the sharing of insights or struggles that seem especially alive. Some may wish to share their collage/sketch from Exercise 2. Continue to encourage prayerful listening for God's Spirit in one another's words.

- In the last few minutes, review this time for themes or patterns that may emerge from shared reflection. Ask what "God clues" these may suggest for the group.

BREAK (10 MINUTES)

DEEPER EXPLORATIONS (45 MINUTES)

Deepening our corporate discernment in relation to the prophetic call

Set the context.

We have been reflecting all week on the prophetic call and elements of suffering or sacrifice that are often the price of fidelity to the prophetic call. The call and the cross are closely connected aspects of our authentic Christian discipleship. Today we will explore a way to open ourselves to a sense of collective call by contemplating God's prayer in us for the church and the world.

Last week we asked what prayer God had placed in us for another person. This week we want to ask what prayer God has placed in us for the world and for a church that witnesses to that world. We will see if we find any pattern in what we hear that might suggest a common call from God to us as a group—a purpose we could carry out of this rich experience together back into our faith community.

Guide a reflection process. (40 minutes)

1. Read Micah 6:8.

- Point to newsprint or chalkboard with three preprinted columns and headings: *Doing Justice, Loving Kindness,* and *Walking Humbly with God.*

- Ask: **Where do we see each aspect of discipleship already alive in some way? Where we can imagine more?** List responses on newsprint. (See Leader's Note, p. 105.)

- Notice which headings are easier to see or imagine examples for.

2. Read Micah 6:8 again.

- Invite members to ponder the question: **What is God's prayer in me for the world?** (Allow three minutes of silence; encourage journaling to clarify and distill the prayer.)

- Share around your circle the prayers heard in each person's heart. Encourage everyone to listen deeply to the prayers they hear, noting in their journals what resonates within them.

- Ask, **Were there any prayers shared where you felt "This seems like God's prayer in *us*"?** (Give sufficient time for all to consider and respond.)

3. Read Micah 6:8 once more.

- Now ask: **What is God's prayer in us for our church, which speaks to our world?** During three minutes of reflection, have people write what they sense in their journal.

- Share your prayers with one another around the circle, listening deeply.

- Ask members to identify patterns or common themes they hear. As leader, take notes on what you hear.

- Can the group name together a sense of God's common call to them from this? Does there seem to be a united spirit of the call here? If so, does a hymn or scripture verse come to mind that captures it?

Take time to debrief the process. (5 minutes)

- What has been valuable or enlightening about this experience?

- What has been surprising or difficult in it?

- Where do we want to go with what we've discovered?

CLOSING (10 MINUTES)

Sing or listen to a song of your choosing. Sing the hymn identified at the end of Deeper Explorations, if one was named.

Read John 15:11. Or read the scripture text identified at the end of Deeper Explorations, if one was cited. Guide a simple examen with the following questions. Invite the group to reflect quietly after each question and jot what they notice in their journals:

- **Where did I sense that we felt joy or energy together in this meeting time?**

- Where did I sense that we felt bored, drained, or anxious in this meeting?

- Do I notice any patterns in how God works with our group?

Invite shared perceptions from the examen; gather them up with the Lord's Prayer.

Remind group of the question adopted for the long term. (If one was not identified, suggest the question: "What is God's yearning for our congregation?") Hand out 3 by 5 cards and have participants print the question on it. Ask the group to stay in touch with each other (perhaps via e-mail) on any responses they receive to this question over the next six months, and to remain open to how God might use their responses for continuing discernment in the body of Christ.

Encourage placing the question in a visible place where it will be seen daily, and taking a few minutes of reflection/journaling with it at regular times.

Remind the group that the final meeting will take fifteen to twenty minutes longer than usual. Offer a closing blessing, using Ephesians 6:24.

Leader's Note

If you need to prompt the group's imagination, especially around the themes of justice and mercy, here are a few possibilities:

- Advocating for prisoners or their families

- Support for survivors of abuse or crime

- Programs to help children and youth understand the roots of discrimination

- Involvement in literacy programs

- Learning and teaching nonviolent communication skills

- Canvassing to discover needs of church members who feel isolated (nursing home residents, homebound persons, members with English language limitations, mothers caring for young children at home)

- Writing letters on behalf of prisoners of conscience

- Connecting gifted retirees with youth in need of mentoring

Feel free to add your own ideas.

Week 10

The All-Encompassing Assurance

PREPARATION

Prepare yourself spiritually. Read the article for Week 10, reflect and journal with the daily exercises, and pray for God's rich blessings on the closure to your small-group experience. Be aware that preparation for this week's meeting may take a bit longer than usual, and stay open to God's guidance as you consider how best to lead the final session. Ask the Holy Spirit to guide each member as you prepare for this last meeting together, and for God to grant you a clear sense of direction in how to share your common learning and practice for the sake of your congregation or faith community.

Prepare the materials and meeting space.

- Check Weekly Needs at a Glance to see items particular to Week 10.

- Arrange chairs in a circle for the Sharing Insights segment, and in a semicircle with a clear area at the front for newsprint or chalkboard for the Deeper Explorations process. This week's worship area might include baptism and Communion symbols—perhaps a bowl or pitcher with water, and chalice/paten/bread/grapes—in addition to the cloth and Christ candle. These central symbols of the church as the body of Christ point to our larger membership and the direction in which we want to take our discernment practice.

- Review the Weekly Meeting. Note that the Opening requires more time than usual, and that Sharing Insights is consequently shortened. Familiarize yourself with the Deeper Explorations process so you can lead comfortably. Review the Leader's Note, adding your own ideas so you can keep the brainstorming segment of Deeper Explorations moving along. This is the segment that will take the group past its normal time frame for the meeting.

- Copy the following illustration onto newsprint or chalkboard for Deeper Explorations:

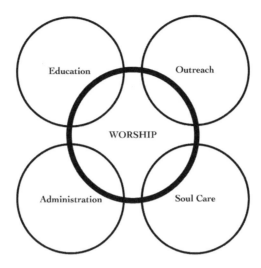

- If using newsprint to list brainstorming ideas (Deeper Explorations), you will need masking tape and a visible area on which to post several newsprint sheets.

- Preprint the quote from Patricia Loring (p. 112) on newsprint/chalkboard for the Closing.

- Make copies of the handout "Liturgy for Discernment" (p. 135) for all participants.

- Select songs/recorded music for the Opening and Closing.

Review the intent of this meeting: to strengthen one another in the assurance of God's continuing presence and guidance throughout our lives, to consider various expressions of discernment in congregational life, and to choose at least one way to bring a discernment practice the group has experienced into the wider life of the church.

OPENING (15 MINUTES—NOTE INCREASE IN TIME)

Welcome participants personally as they enter.

Set the context.

In this, our last meeting for *The Way of Discernment*, we will be looking back on what has been most meaningful in our time together, giving thanks for all the gifts, celebrating God's abiding presence and guidance, and considering how discernment might be woven more deeply into the fabric of our church life. You will notice again that the movement of these ten weeks has gone from personal discernment to practices in community that might benefit the larger church.

Light the Christ candle and offer words like these:

As we bring this journey to a close, we are grateful that the light of Christ has shone upon us in countless ways. We pray it will continue to guide us to the abundant life Jesus came to offer for the sake of the whole world.

Read Jeremiah 29:11-13. Stress the promise that if we seek with all our heart, we will indeed find God. Remind the group: **We have been seeking God's heart for ten weeks now, searching for the way and will of Christ. What have we discovered on this journey?**

Invite quiet reflection on how God has been with us during these ten weeks. Ask: **What were some of the most significant moments that witness to the Spirit's being alive and active among us?** Allow a few minutes of silence for participants to jot notes in their journals.

Invite responses. Encourage each person to name one or two significant moments.

Ask what patterns we might notice. **Looking back, can we see patterns in how God has been with us, or how we've become more aware of God's presence and guidance?** Allow responses to surface slowly from the quiet.

Offer a prayer of thanks for what we have been graced to see together.

Sing a song as blessing. Suggestions: "Take, O Take Me As I Am" (URW #441) or "Leaning on the Everlasting Arms" (UMH #133)

SHARING INSIGHTS (40 MINUTES—NOTE TIME ADJUSTMENT)

During this time, participants share how they have experienced God's presence this past week, drawing especially on responses to the week's reading and daily exercises.

- Encourage everyone to be attentive to God's presence in the group, and what the Spirit may be saying through one another's experiences and remembrances.

- Give participants a few minutes to review their journal entries in response to the week's article and daily exercises.

- Invite the sharing of insights and struggles that seem especially alive. It could be helpful to focus attention on Exercises 3, 4, and 5, inviting members to share their drawings and symbols. If you can willingly model the sharing of your own drawings/symbols, you might take the lead in order to encourage others.

- In the last five minutes, allow time to identify themes or patterns that may offer clues about God's word or guidance for the group.

BREAK (10 MINUTES)

DEEPER EXPLORATIONS (60 MINUTES—NOTE THE LONGER TIME FRAME)

Exploring a call to transformation in the church through discernment

Set the context.

The Way of Discernment has slowly been moving us from a focus on personal practices to group practices and now to the larger picture of discernment in our faith communities. So we want to explore now what it might mean if the church were a community where attention to the Spirit was central and discernment characterized everything the church did. Imagine! What could this look like? And how might our learning here be yeast for transforming our church?

Brainstorming with the Spirit through prayerful imagination (45 minutes)

- Point to the intersecting circles you have drawn on newsprint/chalkboard to represent the five ministry functions: Worship, Education, Soul Care, Outreach, and Administration.[1] Say, **We'll use these five categories to think about discernment at every level of congregational life.** (Be prepared to list responses on a chalkboard or on several sheets of newsprint.)

- Explain the basic process. **This is just a start to gathering ideas and possibilities for the life of the church. We need not make an exhaustive list. Yet a process like this becomes part of our toolbox for corporate discernment, and it can be explored more fully by this group or other church groups in the future.**

- Guide a prayerful brainstorming process, giving eight to ten minutes to each segment. If one area doesn't elicit much response, try a few of your own ideas or suggestions from the Leader's Note.

1. First, let's imagine a church where worship, the heart of congregational life, is shaped by discernment and leads people into discernment. What could allow worship to be more truly an experience of paying attention to the presence and guidance of God?

   Allow a minute or so for people to process the question and begin to imagine responses. Encourage them to jot down ideas. Invite responses, and as they surface, capture them on newsprint/chalkboard in abbreviated words. Feel free to "seed" the sharing with your own ideas or suggestions from the Leader's Note.

2. Next let's imagine a church where the whole education program at every age level expresses discerning wisdom and teaches people how to discern God's way and will in life. Where does the Spirit take us as we try to envision this?

   Again, allow a few minutes for people to begin imagining responses and jotting notes. Capture ideas in shorthand words. Feel free to offer your own ideas or suggestions from the Leader's Note.

3. Now let's imagine a church where all the administrative functions—leadership meetings, decision making, committee life—reflect and promote spiritual discernment. Where do you see the Spirit guiding us here?

   Follow the same pattern for eliciting responses and sharing suggestions.

4. What about a church where soul care (pastoral care) is rooted in discernment, and leads church members needing physical or spiritual care into deeper discernment of God's intention for their lives? What do we imagine here?

   Follow the same pattern for eliciting responses and sharing suggestions.

5. Finally, let's imagine a church where all the outreach in service, mission, and hospitality grows from genuine discernment of God's call. What do you envision?

   Follow the same pattern for eliciting responses and sharing suggestions.

Reflect on the process and God's possible invitation. (10 minutes)

- Which areas elicited ideas readily, and which seemed more difficult to imagine?

- Where do we most sense the energy, excitement, and joy that says: Yes! I'd love to see this in our church?

- Does there seem to be an invitation here from God to our group?

- Where do we feel anxiety or risk? For example, how far are we willing to go down this road?

Making a choice (5 minutes)

- Recall briefly two stories from the chapters in the Participant's Book:

  1. The church board chairwoman who lit a candle and placed an open Bible in their meeting space as a reminder of Christ's presence and way (Week 7)

  2. The farming community church that took up one central question over several years (Week 8)

- What is one place or way we would be willing to try a simple experiment of opening to the Spirit in our congregation? Where do we choose to offer our energies and commitment from this group experience for the larger church?

CLOSING (10 MINUTES)

Sing or listen to a song of your choosing.
> Suggestion: "May You Run and Not Be Weary" (URW #451)

Offer spontaneous prayers of thanks and praise for gifts/blessings/new directions.

Read Matthew 28:18-20. Repeat the last sentence. Pause briefly and repeat it again.
Remind the group that:

- God *has been with us* from our birth until now, and certainly through these ten weeks together;

- God *is with us now* in our choices of where to take our learning;

- God *will continue to be with us* as we take small steps into our future, attentive to the Spirit of grace.

Read together the following quote from Patricia Loring, a Quaker writer, on discernment:

> Co-creation implies a still unfolding creation
> in which the Creator continues to work with and through us
> when we respond in faithfulness
> to the promptings of Love and Truth in our hearts.[2]

Point out that all discernment is part of this co-creative process with God, our spirits opening to the Holy Spirit and choosing to work with the direction and guidance we receive. Invite each person to continue this co-creative venture with the living God!

Remind the group of the question adopted for the long term (at the previous meeting). Encourage group members to stay in touch with one another on any responses they feel they might be receiving to this question over time, and to stay open to how God may use this question for the sake of the body of Christ or the larger human community.

Sing or listen to a closing song as a benediction.

    Suggestions:

    "Go in Peace, Walk in Love" (URW #444)

    "Jesus, My God and My All" (URW #423)

    "Go Now in Peace" or "Dona Nobis Pacem" (traditional rounds; "Dona Nobis Pacem"
       is found in UMH #665)

Leader's Note

IDEAS FOR FOSTERING DISCERNMENT IN CONGREGATIONAL LIFE

WORSHIP

- Give a minute or two of silence after the scripture reading or sermon for people to absorb and hear more deeply how God is speaking to them through the Word.

- Invite the pastor to let sermon preparation grow out of group *lectio*. (See p. 73 for instructions on group *lectio*.) Or, instead of a traditional sermon, the pastor may lead a modified group *lectio* with the Gospel for the day.

- Before the benediction, give congregants a chance to ponder where and how God has touched their hearts in the service, and how they feel moved to respond.

- Invite your church's worship committee to take time to discern kinds of music needed by members with different personalities and musical preferences.

Add your own ideas.

EDUCATION

- Encourage your Christian education committee to use discernment in the process of selecting appropriate resources for children, youth, and adults.

- Select resources that teach church members at various stages of development how to listen more closely to God and one another.

- Get adults, youth, and children involved in the Holy Listening exercise (p. 34), each in their own learning settings. This exercise could be repeated at regular internals.

- Bring some discernment practices learned here into classes (determine which ones are appropriate).

- Encourage more small-group learning and spiritual growth opportunities.

Add your own ideas.

ADMINISTRATION

- Structure meetings of your governing board/trustees/deacons as worshipful work, incorporating scriptural reflection; faith sharing; and silence to listen to the Spirit's guidance at critical moments of impasse, conflict, uncertainty. (Offer the appendix "Liturgy for Discernment," p. 135, as one example of how a meeting may be structured as worship.)

- Ask church committees to identify a long-term question to live into over time, a question central to their function in the body of Christ.

- Encourage your church staff and leaders to have an annual spiritual retreat for discerning larger issues/long-term directions for the church.

- As a group, ask to meet with pastoral staff and church leaders to discuss ideas.

Add your own ideas.

SOUL CARE

- Learn to be present to God and to others in silence. Simple, quiet presence is a form of soul care for the confused and grieving. This ministry, belonging to the whole congregation, opens space for discernment of need and response.

- Pay attention to the special needs of your congregation and larger community over time. Who in the community around us cry out for Jesus' love? What do people suffer from: economic pressures, loss of meaning, addiction, abuse, mental illness?

- Open up healing spaces in worship, small groups, and retreats where people can experience grace in new ways and begin to hear deeper callings in life.

- Teach the Clearness Committee process for persons needing guidance on important life decisions.

Add your own ideas.

OUTREACH

- Encourage outreach/service committees first to discern with their congregation's help where the deepest community needs lie; then discern where their gifts/energy/joy are called forth in relation to them.

- Invite old and new members to take a spiritual gifts inventory; connect them to church ministries that use their true gifts, not just their abilities (so energy is maintained, not depleted).

- Collect stories of people and congregations who discerned their true calling in the world. Post on bulletin boards and use in classes and committee meetings to inspire personal and corporate discernment.

Add your own ideas.

Notes

PREPARATORY MEETING

Holy Listening Exercise: The quotation at the top of this page is from Eugene H. Peterson, *Working the Angles: The Shape of Pastoral Integrity* (Grand Rapids, MI: William B. Eerdmans Publishing, 1987), 103–104.

WEEK 2

1. Gerald G. May, *Will and Spirit: A Contemplative Psychology* (San Francisco: Harper & Row Publishers, 1982), 290.

2. "Psalm Prayer (Ps. 25)," adapted by Judy Holloway, in *Upper Room Worshipbook: Music and Liturgies for Spiritual Formation* (Nashville: Upper Room Books, 2006), no. 249.

WEEK 3

1. Cited in *The United Methodist Hymnal* (Nashville: The United Methodist Publishing House, 1989), no. 493.

2. "Psalm Prayer (Ps. 1)," adapted by Douglas Mills, in *Upper Room Worshipbook,* no. 225.

WEEK 4

1. "Psalm Prayer (Ps. 139)," adapted by Irenaeus (2nd century), in *Upper Room Worshipbook,* no. 348.

WEEK 5

1. Dag Hammarskjöld, *Markings,* trans. Leif Sjöberg and W. H. Auden (New York: Alfred A. Knopf, 1964), 90.

WEEK 8

1. The Shalem Institute, located in Bethesda, Maryland, teaches both individual and group spiritual direction. For more information, see www.shalem.org.

WEEK 10

1. Kent Ira Groff identifies these five "ministry functions" in *The Soul of Tomorrow's Church: Weaving Spiritual Practices in Ministry Together* (Nashville: Upper Room Books, 2000), 39.

2. Patricia Loring, *Listening Spirituality,* vol. 2 (Washington, DC: Openings Press, 1999), 69.

Appendix

See also "Steps for Prayerful Discernment" in foundational *Companions in Christ*, Part 5, Week 4 Leader's Note (adapted from *Discerning God's Will Together* by Danny E. Morris and Charles M. Olsen [Nashville: Upper Room Books, 1997]), 66–67.

Living into the Answers: A Workbook for Personal Spiritual Discernment by Valerie K. Isenhower and Judith A. Todd is available from Upper Room Books. This workbook contains exercises based on the Morris-Olsen model for those who wish to work with one approach in a more systematic way.

Ignatian Teachings on Discernment

What Is Ignatian Spirituality? Essence and Experience

by Tim Malone

Many times we have been asked: What exactly is Ignatian spirituality? What essence and experience distinguish this spirituality from another? Concretely, how may I experience this process without going on a thirty-day silent retreat? Let's look at the hallmarks of Ignatian spirituality and explore ways to live it out in our daily lives.

Ignatian spirituality flows out of the Catholic Christian tradition. At its roots, though, it is ecumenical in nature—its origin and aim are ultimately about encountering the living spirit of God, whatever one's tradition. That is what happened 450 years ago to Ignatius of Loyola, a sixteenth-century Spanish noble warrior. While [he was] on a passionate quest to find God, the God of love *found him.* Out of these life-changing experiences came the *Spiritual Exercises of Saint Ignatius,* the methods Ignatius would give to laypersons and clergy alike so they might become transformed, freed to love. Only after this experience and seeking a way to serve did Ignatius then choose the path of priesthood and found a religious order. Here are some hallmarks of Ignatian spirituality as translated for our modern day:

- This "pathway to God" has endured over the centuries, not so much as a particular prayer style as *a way of attending to personal experiences.* That is, our senses, feelings, even our deepest desires become privileged places to discover God's dynamic presence leading us— to become whole; to become our authentic, "true" selves—in short, to grow in relationship to ourselves, God, and our community.

- The Spirit that totally animated Jesus' life is available to all who would open their lives to receive. How? By "taking a long, loving look" at Jesus' life and his particular way of being in the world, God reveals to us mysteries of *who we are* as human beings as well.

- Through reflection on his own pattern of life choices, Ignatius developed an approach to human decision making based on "discernment of spirits." As Peter Byrne, SJ notes, "We can detect and discern the movement of spirits (God's and others competing for our allegiance) and make choices most conducive to the Divine Purpose." Freed from fear and false attachments, we are made more available to offer ourselves, in love, to the source of Love, and to serve from that place within of heart and healed soul.

Adapted from www.ignatiancenter.org; reprinted with permission of the Ignatian Spirituality Center Newsletter Archives, info@ignatiancenter.org.

Discerning through Reason and Imagination

In *Hearing with the Heart*, Debra K. Farrington takes direction from the *Spiritual Exercises of Saint Ignatius*, written in the sixteenth century. Ignatius gave guidelines for using both reason (the list of pros and cons) and imagination (waiting on God) to listen for God's call. The following is excerpted from *Hearing with the Heart*:

- Step one, Ignatius wrote, is to **put the matter before yourself clearly.** What are you trying to discern? What is your question? The more clearly you define the question, the better your hopes of coming to a clear conclusion.

  It is so simple to spend a lot of time focused on the wrong question. By putting your issue or question down in black and white or at least exploring it thoroughly in your thoughts or in conversation with others and being aware of its background, it is possible to discover facets of the decision that have never occurred to you. You may even discover that the question you thought was uppermost in your mind isn't the right question after all.

- Ignatius' second step is to **remain open and objective about the possibilities.**

  We are not likely to be without a preference for one outcome or the other; rather, we are like the contestant on a game show who wants God to pick door number one. But as much as possible, try to remain open to all possibilities. You never know what bit of evidence may tip the scales in an unexpected way.

- The third step in Ignatius' system is to **pray to God to move our will so that we can know what we should do.** We don't rely on our own resources in discernment, but we pray for God's guidance and the will to follow it. This isn't as easy as it sounds; it is easy to say a prayer and ask for guidance and the will to follow through, but it can be difficult to put aside our own willfulness and desire for a specific outcome.

- Making a list and checking it twice: All three of the steps just described, part of Ignatius' first method, help prepare us for a balanced discernment process. Next, Ignatius asks us to focus specifically on our reasoning skills. Ignatius suggests that we **make a pro-and-con list for the choices before us.** Some questions you might consider while making that list include these:

  - What will be gained in choosing each of the paths before you?

  - What will be lost by rejecting any of the choices?

- How do the choices benefit others?

- In what ways do the choices inconvenience or disrupt the lives of others?

- What excites you most about the options? What do you look forward to?

- What would you dislike if you picked one path or the other?

- What are your motivations for choosing one option or another?

- Ignatius' fourth step is to **examine that list you made and "see to which side reason more inclines."** The last two two steps of Ignatius focus on reason alone. It is impossible to separate reason from feeling completely, but Ignatius asks us to do that as much as we can and put feelings or imagination aside for the moment.

- At this point, you are ready to take the final step in Ignatius' first method for making a sound discernment, which is to **take your conclusions to God in prayer and, with open heart, ask for confirmation or guidance** that your discernment is correct.

Ignatius' second method of making a good discernment has us turning away from reason for a while and using our imagination to explore the options before us.

- As with his first method, Ignatius begins by reminding us to **approach the decisions clearly, with a solid sense of the issue to be explored.** Then, with the love of God uppermost in our thoughts, we try to **practice indifference to the outcome.**

- Once we have prepared ourselves in this way, Ignatius suggests that we imagine three different scenarios. First, imagine that someone comes to you with the same dilemma you face and asks your advice.

- What questions would you ask, and how would that imaginary person answer you? Try to get a sense of how you think this person is feeling and how that influences the advice you would give. Keeping uppermost in your mind your desire for the person to choose the dream of God, what path would you recommend taking?

- Next, Ignatius asks us to imagine ourselves on our own deathbed, looking back at the decision we are now trying to make. What path do you wish you had chosen?

- Pay close attention to how you feel emotionally and physically as you imagine these scenarios. Does one give you a greater sense of energy, enthusiasm, or peacefulness (feelings of consolation)? Or does one of them cause tension, tightness in your body, anxiety, anger, or resentment (feelings of desolation)?

- Finally, Ignatius suggests that we **consider ourselves on the final judgment day ... face-to-face with God, who loves [us], reviewing the choices [we] have made.** Try to imagine what you would say to God and how it would feel to review the choices you have made. Of the choices before you, is there one that you would find easiest to speak to God about? Which would you rather not discuss with God? Which path do you think will bring you into a deeper relationship or responsiveness to God? Finally, which option do you believe is the clearest choice for you as God's loving agent in the world?

After exploring these three imaginary scenarios and noticing your feelings and bodily responses, you may have a clearer sense of the path to choose.

From Debra K. Farrington, *Hearing with the Heart: A Gentle Guide to Discerning God's Will for Your Life* (San Francisco: Jossey-Bass, 2003), 144–157. Reprinted with permission of John Wiley & Sons Inc.

Teresa of Ávila's Criteria for Discernment of Spirits

A list of signs to the soul that indicate clearly
whether or not an experience is of God

1. A word that comes to you from God will have the authority (power) to *effect* what it says.

2. Such a word will remain indelibly imprinted on the memory with great certitude.

3. Any vision or word that is truly of God will leave deep peace, tranquility, and joy in the soul (beneath the turbulent change of surface emotions).

4. A spiritual experience that is of God, no matter how extraordinary, results in greater humility and a deeper awareness of our own weakness, limitation, and sin.

5. Such experiences make us long not to offend God ("grieve the Holy Spirit") in any way; we become deeply pained even by our potential for unintended sin.

6. Authentic divine grace leads to a deeper desire to serve God without reward, and to suffer for God's sake if it will bring God greater glory.

7. A true mark of the Divine Presence in the soul is a burning desire to love and praise God, and to see every other creature love and praise God as God deserves.

Cautions relating to mystical graces in prayer:

• Never seek them out; they are to be received only as gift.

• Do not give them credence automatically; test the spirits.

• Do not imagine yourself better than others if you receive such graces.

Developed by Marjorie J. Thompson; based on Teresa of Ávila's *Interior Castle.*

The Clearness Committee: A Communal Approach to Discernment

Parker J. Palmer

Many of us face a series of difficult dilemmas when we are trying to deal with a personal problem, question, or decision. On the one hand, we know that the issue is ours alone to resolve and we believe that we have the inner resources to resolve it—but those resources are often hidden from us by layers of inner "stuff." On the other hand, we know that other people might help us discover our resources and find our way—but by exposing our problem to others, we run the risk of being invaded by their judgments, assumptions, and advice—a common and painful experience. As a result, we too often privatize these vital questions in our lives. At the very moment when we need all the help we can get, we find ourselves cut off from our own inner resources *and* the resources of a community.

For people who have experienced these dilemmas, I want to describe a method invented by the Quakers, a method that protects individual identity and integrity while drawing on the wisdom of other people. It is called a "Clearness Committee." If that name sounds like it is from the sixties, it is—the 1660s! From their beginnings over three hundred years ago, Quakers needed a way to draw on both inner and communal resources to deal with personal problems because they had no clerical leaders to "solve" their problems for them. The Clearness Committee is testimony to the fact that there are no external authorities on life's deepest issues, not clergy or therapists or scholars; there is only the authority that lies within each of us waiting to be heard.

Behind the Clearness Committee is a simple but crucial conviction: *each of us has an inner teacher, a voice of truth, that offers the guidance and power we need to deal with our problems.* But that inner voice is often garbled by various kinds of inward and outward interference. The function of the Clearness Committee is not to give advice or "fix" people from the outside in, but to help people remove the interference so that they can discover their own wisdom from the inside out. If we do not believe in the reality of inner wisdom, the Clearness Committee can become an opportunity for manipulation. But if we respect the power of the inner teacher, the Clearness Committee can be a remarkable way to help someone name and claim his or her deepest truth.

The Clearness Committee's work is guided by some simple but crucial rules and understandings. Among these, of course, is the rule that *the process is confidential.* When it is over, committee members will not speak with others about what was said—and they will not speak with the focus person about the problem unless he or she requests a conversation.

1. Normally, the person who seeks clearness (the "focus person") chooses his or her committee—a minimum of five and a maxium of six trusted people with as much diversity among them as possible in age, background, gender, etc.

2. The focus person writes up his or her issue in four to six pages and sends this document to members of the committee in advance of the meeting. There are three sections to this write-up: a concise *statement of the problem*, a recounting of *relevant background factors* that may bear on the problem, and an exploration of any hunches the focus person may have about *what's on the horizon* regarding the problem. Most people find that by writing a statement of this sort, they are taking their first step toward inner clearness.

3. The committee meets for three hours—with the understanding that there may be a need for a second or third meeting at a later date. A clerk (facilitator) and a recording clerk (secretary) should be named, though taping the meeting is a good alternative to the latter. The clerk opens the meeting with a reminder of the rules, closes the meeting on time, and serves as a monitor all along the way, making sure that the rules are followed with care. The recording clerk gives his or her notes to the focus person when the meeting is over.

4. The meeting begins with the clerk calling for a time of centering silence and inviting the focus person to break the silence, when ready, with a brief oral summary of the issue at hand. Then the committee members may speak—but everything they say is governed by one rule, a simple rule and yet one that most people find difficult and demanding: members are forbidden to speak to the focus person in any way except to ask honest, open questions. This means absolutely no advice and no amateur psychoanalysis. It means no ,"Why don't you . . . ?" It means no, "That happened to me one time, and here's what I did. . . . " It means no, "There's a book/therapist/exercise/diet that would help you a lot." Nothing is allowed except *real* questions, honest and open questions, questions that will help the focus person remove the blocks to his or her inner truth without becoming burdened by the personal agendas of committee members. I may think I know the answer to your problem, and on rare occasions I may be right. But *my* answer is of absolutely no value to you. The only answer that counts is one that arises from your own inner truth. The discipline of the Clearness Committee is to give you greater access to that truth—and to keep the rest of us from defiling or trying to define it.

5. What is an honest, open question? It is important to reflect on this, since we are so skilled at asking questions that are advice or analysis in disguise: "Have you ever thought that it might be your mother's fault?" The best single mark of an honest, open question is that the questioner could not possibly know the answer to it: "Did you ever feel like this before?"

There are other guidelines for good questioning. *Ask questions aimed at serving the focus person* rather than at satisfying your curiosity. *Ask questions that are brief and to the point* rather than larding them with background considerations and rationale—which make the questions into a speech. *Ask questions that go to the person as well as the problem*—e.g., questions about feelings as well as about facts. Trust your intuition in asking questions, even if your instinct seems off the wall: "What color is your present job, and what color is the one you have been offered?"

6. Normally, the focus person responds to the questions as they are asked, in the presence of the group, and those responses generate more, and deeper, questions. Though the responses should be full, they should not be terribly long—resist the temptation to tell your life story in response to every question! It is important that there be time for more and more questions and responses, thus deepening the process for everyone. The more often a focus person is willing to answer aloud, the more material he or she, and the committee, will have to work with. But this should never happen at the expense of the focus person's need to protect vulnerable feelings or to maintain privacy. It is vital that the focus person assume total power to set the limits of the process. So the second major rule of the Clearness Committee is this: *it is always the focus person's right not to answer a question.* The unanswered question is not necessarily lost—indeed, it may be the question that is so important that it keeps working on the focus person long after the Clearness Committee has ended.

7. The Clearness Committee must not become a grilling, a cross-examination. The pace of the questioning is crucial—it should be relaxed, gentle, humane. A machine-gun fire of questions makes reflection impossible and leaves the focus person feeling invaded rather than evoked. Do not be afraid of silence in the group—trust it and treasure it. When silence falls, it does not mean that nothing is happening or that the process has broken down. It may well mean that the most important thing of all is happening—new insights are emerging from within people, from their deepest sources of guidance.

8. From beginning to end of the Clearness Committee, it is important that everyone work hard to remain totally attentive to the focus person and his or her needs. This means suspending the normal rules of social gatherings—no chitchat, no responding to other people's questions or to the focus person's answers, no joking to break the tension, no noisy and nervous laughter to indicate that we "get it." We are simply to surround the focus person with quiet, loving space, resisting even the temptation to comfort or reassure or encourage this person, but simply being present with our attention and our questions and our care. If a committee member damages this ambiance with advice, leading questions, or rapid-fire inquisition, other members—including the focus person—should remind that person

of the rules, and he or she should not argue the point. The Clearness Committee is for the focus person; the rest of us need to learn to recede.

9. The Clearness Committee should run for the full time allotted. Don't end early for fear that the group has "run out of questions"—patient waiting will be rewarded with deeper questions than have yet been asked. About thirty minutes before the end of the meeting, the clerk should ask the focus person if he or she wants to suspend the "questions only" rule and invite committee members to mirror back what they have heard the focus person saying. If the focus person says no, the questions continue, but if he or she says yes, mirroring can begin, along with more questions. "Mirroring" does not provide an excuse to give advice or "fix" the person—that sort of invasiveness is still prohibited. Mirroring simply means reflecting back the focus person's own words and behavior to see if he or she can say, "Yes, that's me . . ." or "No, that's not. . . ." In the final ten minutes of the meeting, the clerk should invite members to celebrate and affirm the focus person and his or her strengths. This is an important time, since the focus person has just spent a couple of hours feeling vulnerable. And there is always much to celebrate, for in the course of a Clearness Committee, people reveal the gifts and graces that characterize human beings at their deepest and best.

10. Remember, the Clearness Committee is not intended to "fix" the focus person, so there should be no sense of letdown if the focus person does not have his or her problems "solved" when the process ends. A good clearness process does not end—it keeps working within the focus person long after the meeting is over. The rest of us need simply to keep holding that person in the light, trusting the wisdom of his or her inner teacher.

The Clearness Committee is not a cure-all. It is not for extremely fragile people or for extremely delicate problems. But for the right person, with the right issue, it is a powerful way to rally the strength of community around a struggling soul, to draw deeply from the wisdom within all of us. It teaches us to abandon the pretense that we know what is best for another person and instead to ask those honest and open questions that can help that person find his or her own answers. It teaches us to give up the arrogant assumption that we are obliged to "save" each other, and learn, through simple listening, to create the conditions that allow a person to find his or her wholeness within. If the spiritual discipline behind the Clearness Committee is understood and practiced, the process can become a way to renew community in our individualistic times, a way to free people from their isolation without threatening their integrity, a way to counteract the excesses of techniques in caring, a way to open new channels for the Spirit to move among us with healing and power.

An Exercise in Listening to God

Compose yourself in quiet.

Relax.

Breathe deeply and gently.

Re-collect yourself before God.

Ponder a significant question you have about your life (not an abstract question).

Pose your question to God. It may help to imagine asking Jesus.

Be in silence, open to what comes. Don't try to think up an answer.

Allow images, impressions, words, feelings, intuitions to surface.

If insights arise, note them on paper.

If nothing comes, don't worry. Try one of these:

- Go for a walk with no agenda.
- Pick up clay, paper and crayons, or some creative medium and just play.
- Journal a dialogue: allow an interior conversation to unfold between you and God/Jesus/Spirit.

If something comes to you as gift, give thanks!

If you think you might have gotten a clue, pray to stay alert to further signs.

If nothing discernible happened, ask to hear/see what you need over the next few days.

Process developed by Marjorie J. Thompson.

Examen Before Sleep

The examen is a basic form of discernment in daily life. Ask yourself the following questions.

1. Where have I experienced energy and joy in this day?

2. Where have I felt drained or anxious in this day?

3. Where have I felt near to God in the activities and decisions of the day?

4. Where have I felt distant from God in the day?

Let your prayer flow spontaneously from what surfaces out of these questions.

Listening Together to a Key Question

(20–25 minutes)

The intent here is to give people a chance to listen for God's leading, first within themselves and then collectively, and to begin to sense, sort, and sift where this leading may be taking them. The process works best for groups of three to six, so please brief other leaders on the process if your group is larger than six persons. It is simple to lead:

• Invite your group into quiet, simply opening to the presence of God in your midst.

• After a minute or so, ask the question that has surfaced for the group. Invite people to reflect prayerfully on this question.

• After a few minutes of silence, ask participants to let inner responses to the question condense into a single word or phrase, no more than a sentence.

• Then invite each person to (1) speak the word or phrase that has come to her or him, without elaboration; (2) listen prayerfully to what each other person offers.

• After all have spoken, invite silence for all to hear the echoes.

• As the group continues in silence, ask all to consider quietly, "What theme or Voice have you perhaps begun to hear speaking beneath and through all that has been shared?"

• After another few minutes of silence, ask participants to share with one another what may be surfacing in answer to this question.

• Allow several minutes for sharing. Acknowledge that new understandings may continue to emerge, and invite the group back into quiet. Close with a simple prayer of thanksgiving for any fresh insights that have arisen.

Review the experience. (5 minutes)

• Invite participants to reflect on their experience of the quiet, the listening, the simplicity of speaking few words, and insights that may have begun to emerge.

• Name what you have done as a simple beginning to corporate discernment. Encourage participants to keep listening for answers that may surface over time in relation to this question.

Process developed by Stephen V. Doughty.

Forms of Deliberation

Compiled by Victoria G. Curtiss

Debate	Dialogue	Discernment
One side knows "the truth" and seeks to persuade others to join its way of thinking	Understanding or direction emerges through listening to many or all the voices in the group	A community of believers seeks the Holy Spirit's guidance through prayer; reflection on scripture, tradition, values, and current realities; dialogue; and finding places of agreement
Defends a viewpoint	Suspends judgment	Offers "holy indifference"
Uses advocacy, persuasion	Balances advocacy with inquiry; explores underlying assumptions, causes, rules	Takes a "long, loving look at the real"—contemplation
Uses hard data to get answers to problems; reasoning is made explicit	Seeks to get to deeper questions and possibly new framing of issues	Uses intellect/reason and affect/intuition: mind and spirit experience
Resolves by defeating or persuading opposing side; or may find synthesis of opposites	Invents unprecedented possibilities and new insights; produces a collective flow	Uncovers a decision rather than making it; discovers what is most life-giving/loving by listening to wisdom of the Spirit and all voices
Distinguishes and polarizes differences	Looks for what exists between extremes of differences	Seeks to hold polarities in balance
Sees parts, may seek connection among them	Looks for coherence first	Builds on belief that all are part of one body of Christ
Persons identify with positions or stay in fixed roles	Conversation uncovers concerns, needs, fears, hopes, interests	Options are weighed apart from being identified with particular persons
Each side names strengths of its own position and weaknesses of the other	Group members work together to name strengths and weaknesses of all options	Group members name the negatives of an option, then the positives
Either/or choices: binary	Multiple options	May generate multiple options, discover a "third way," or discern yes or no
Knower's mind	Learner's mind	Seeker's mind

COMMUNAL DISCERNMENT

Spiritual communal discernment involves a community of faith distinguishing between what is of God and what is not. It may include these steps:

1. **Establish a common starting point** through clarifying the issue and guiding principles, building relationships, worshiping and praying together, and remembering a shared faith heritage.

2. **Gather and share information** through study of the Bible, history, theology, polity, and church practices; and listening to the experiences, hopes, and concerns of those affected by the outcome.

3. **Explore options** with the whole group naming alternatives and working as one body to weigh the negatives and positives of each option, with prayerful reflection throughout.

4. **Choose direction** based on emerging consensus in the group.

5. **Rest with the decision** for a time to make sure it continues to seem the right direction.

"Forms of Deliberation" and steps of "Communal Discernment" are reprinted by permission. For further information, see *Guidelines for Communal Discernment* by Victoria G. Curtiss (Louisville, KY: Office of the General Assembly and the Peacemaking Program of the Presbyterian Church [USA], 2008). Order through Presbyterian Distribution Services at 800-524-2612.

Skills for Group Discernment

Our goal is to hear God's will together in order to allow Jesus Christ to lead his church. To listen well, we need to practice certain disciplines:

1. Settle yourself in God's presence. Lay aside any distracting concerns and invite the Holy Spirit to help you be open to the voice and desires of God.

2. Listen to others with all of your senses (your feelings and intuition as well as your reason).

3. Speak only for yourself, referring to your experiences, thoughts, and feelings (as opposed to speaking for others who aren't present).

4. Do not interrupt or challenge what others say. Allow the Holy Spirit to layer "good ideas upon good ideas" and to bring to our collective awareness the key values for us to consider.

5. Do not formulate what you are going to say while someone else is speaking.

6. Allow a little silence after each person speaks. Use this silence to prayerfully consider what has been said.

7. Leave space for those who haven't yet contributed to the conversation before speaking a second time.

8. Listen to the whole group, to those who have not spoken as well as to those who have. Listen for how the Spirit is leading the group through all of the ideas suggested.

Adapted by John E. Anderson from Suzanne G. Farnham, Stephanie A. Hull, and R. Taylor McLean, "Discernment Listening Guidelines," in *Grounded in God: Listening Hearts Discernment for Group Deliberations* (Harrisburg, PA: Morehouse Publishing, 1996), 55. Used by permission.

Stages of Group Discernment

1. Quiet ourselves of any distractions and open ourselves to the Spirit's leading.

2. Define the issue before us. Ask any clarifying questions.

3. Clarify how our life experiences may influence our ability to hear God's voice on this topic.

4. Commit to a "holy indifference" as to how the living Christ might resolve this.

5. Brainstorm together about scriptures that may speak to this issue. Choose one or two passages to reflect on as a group.

6. Read the selected scripture(s), reflecting personally on insights gained from them.

7. Glean together any wisdom discerned from our reflection on God's Word.

8. Suggest possible resolutions that may emerge out of our listening to the complexity of this issue, our own past experiences, scripture and biblical principles, or insights from the Christian tradition.

9. Come to a consensus on a resolution that honors all of the above concerns.

Based on *Discerning God's Will Together: A Spiritual Practice for the Church* by Danny E. Morris and Charles M. Olsen (Nashville: Upper Room Books, 1997).

Participating in God's Revealing

Abiding in the presence of God is the context in which this process is experienced. Stop at each critical point to heed inner prompting. Trust the process. Realize this may be a cyclical journey, and you may return to any step at any time.

1. **ASKING**—Center in prayer. Allow a question to take shape beginning with *what*, not *how, when, which, who,* or *why.* The intention is to reveal "What is ours to do?"

2. **ALIGNING**—Identify the guiding principles and values that are important here. What is your credo? your vision/mission statement or spiritual principles/beliefs/values?

3. **RELEASING**—Specify impeding thoughts, assumptions, experiences, fears, or agendas. What must we release to participate freely in God's revealing?

4. **PROCLAIMING**—Affirm faith in the Spirit's work within each person, and trust in the reality of divine guidance among you.

5. **CONTRIBUTING**—Declare your gifts. Ask, "What do I bring, as an individual, that I am willing to offer?"

6. **FOCUSING**—Arrive at one clear question. It is the vehicle for the remainder of the process. The underlying question: "What is ours to do at this time?"

7. **RECEIVING**—Take the question into silence. "Be still and know." Clearly articulate responses received without judging or giving much detail.

8. **CONVERGING**—Cluster responses according to their common themes. Around which concept(s) does the group energy gravitate?

9. **EXPANDING**—Exercise your power of imagination to "be there now." What does each emergent concept look and feel like, expanded to its ultimate expression?

10. **UNIFYING**—Reflecting on the expanded concept(s), create a statement that supports moving forward.

11. **ANCHORING**—Embrace an anchor. What biblical text, image, symbol, song, quote, or affirmation roots us in the truth of this experience?

12. **IMPLEMENTING**—Take action. Who will do what, by when? (See step 5, Contributing.)

Celebrate! Share the joy with the community. Be grateful, communicative, and mindful as the plan unfolds.

Co-created at New World Unity Church; originally titled "Participating in God's Unfolding." For more information on individual or group discernment, visit www.newworldunity.org or call (703) 913-8560.

Liturgy for Discernment

"Let . . . God show us where we should go and what we should do" (Jer. 42:3).

RITUAL

Silence, song, lighting a candle . . . recognizing God in our midst

RELATING

Attending to each other: How and where are you?

RECEIVING

Attending to God prayerfully: lectio divina, *awareness examen, guided imagery*

RUMINATING

Sharing what we notice during the prayer time

REFLECTING

Connecting with our sense of call or mission: What is God's invitation?

RESPONDING

From our listening, turning to our work/decision making/business at hand

RETURNING

Closing with prayer, thanksgiving, offering of self and effort to God

Adapted from resource by Mark Yaconelli, author of *Contemplative Youth Ministry: Practicing the Presence of Jesus* (Grand Rapids, MI: Zondervan, 2006.) Earlier version used by permission in 2004 Companions in Christ trainings.

Discernment: To See as God Sees

James 1:5-6   1 Kings 3:5, 9-14   Romans 12:2   Ephesians 5:15-17

Three Preconditions to Discernment

1. Have a relationship of open communication with God.

2. Have a desire to know the will of God.

3. Have a commitment to do the will of God.

Steps for Corporate Discernment (developed by Bishop David J. Lawson)

1. Gather good data and basic factual information, identifying alternatives and possibilities.

2. Insist that all categories be kept "soft" [fluid] in order that creativity may be present and contribute to the process.

3. Maintain a holy indifference to the outcome, laying aside all biases and prejudices. Be willing to leave the outcome to God's direction and be obedient to the results.

4. Maintain a community and climate of worship.

5. Ask and respond to the question, "Where have we sensed God's affirmation in what we have been about?"

6. Spend time in reflection and prayer, listening to God's intimations in the future, hints of God's direction.

7. Share with the faith community what you have seen, heard, and felt in your reflection time. Dialogue about it. At this stage there is no right or wrong, but rather a desire to hear God. Frequently, insight and wisdom come in the dialogue.

8. Humility is crucial. Each person must be constantly aware that God may have spoken through someone else.

9. Wait for God's timing. Honor silence when it comes. Continue to seek God's direction as you wait.

10. Be willing to receive new ideas and consider them, keeping a holy indifference to the outcome.

11. When consensus begins to form, continue to offer all plans and commitment to God for reshaping.

How did the early church reach a consensus?

1. They allowed the Holy Spirit to be their guide.

2. They devoted themselves to prayer, teaching, and the Lord's Supper (Acts 2:42).

3. They were one in heart and mind (Acts 4:32).

Adapted from a resource developed by the Rev. Jessica Moffatt Seay. "Steps for Corporate Discernment" were written by Bishop David J. Lawson and published in the *Ministry Inquiry Process*. Copyright © 1997 (updated 2004) by the General Board of Higher Education and Ministry, The United Methodist Church. Used by permission.

Graced Communal History

This process may be especially useful when discerning divine guidance in relation to divisive issues that leave many congregations and denominations in serious conflict.

Graced Communal History assists a group to become aware of the impact of its past on its current life, recognizing the movement of the Holy Spirit through consolations (peace, vitality, joy) and desolations (discomfort, loss, sadness). It was developed by Father John English, who taught that there is always consensus in a group, and the issue is to discover that consensus.[1]

One way to discern is through memory. The premise of Graced History is that one's personal graced history is within communal history, which is within God's salvation history. God is present in each person's life story and also in the history of a community/group. This history can be reflected upon in the context of God's constant, loving presence. The three classic movements within salvation history are *grace, sin,* and *resurrection hope.* There may be overlap among the three categories.

1. Each participant spends from thirty to sixty minutes in personal prayer reflecting on the following questions:

   a. How have you encountered God's grace (forgiveness, liberation, reconciliation, restoration, cleansing, homecoming, blessing) as you have engaged the identified issue—whether through the study of scripture, life encounters with others, or membership in a local church or denomination experiencing conflict over this issue?

   b. How have you encountered sin (exile, disobedience, bondage, constricted vision, judgment, separation from God and others)—in your own life as well as elsewhere—having been part of a church that struggles with this issue?

   c. In the midst of your church's struggle, what signs of resurrection have you encountered (dying and rising, hope, forward movement, drawing good out of evil, creating new life)—points at which God is working in you and through our common struggle to bring new life?

2. The group reconvenes, and each person takes a turn addressing the three questions, one at a time. There is no interaction except asking questions for clarification. At the end of each person's sharing, the speaker tells the scribe what words will capture his or her thoughts

on a large piece of paper with this title written at the top: The History Line. The scribe uses different colors for thoughts related to grace, sin, and resurrection. Other participants may speak as they feel moved to do so. Silence is fine; let it invite sharing. The facilitator and scribe are also afforded an opportunity to speak.

3. After all who desire have shared, the whole group is subdivided into smaller groups in which members discuss what common themes or dimensions they observe from all the sharing. Each subgroup reports these for further reflection on what themes are common among all the subgroups. These are recorded as learnings or affirmations upon which all can agree.

---

1. John English (1924–2004) was a Jesuit priest who expanded the use of the *Spiritual Exercises of Saint Ignatius* for group discernment. He taught at the Guelph Centre of Spirituality in Guelph, Canada.

Adapted from material developed by Rev. Victoria Curtiss. Used by permission. To order Rev. Curtiss's booklet *Guidelines to Communal Discernment,* contact Presbyterian Distribution Services at 800-524-2612.

Credits

"A Process for Group *Lectio*," adapted from *Gathered in the Word: Praying the Scripture in Small Groups* by Norvene Vest © 1996. Used by permission of Upper Room Books.

 "Psalm Prayer (Ps. 25)," adapted by Judy Holloway, in *Upper Room Worshipbook: Music and Liturgies for Spiritual Formation* © 2006. Used by permission of Upper Room Books.

"Psalm Prayer (Ps. 1)," adapted by Douglas Mills, in *Upper Room Worshipbook* © 2006. Used by permission of Upper Room Books.

"Psalm Prayer (Ps. 139)," adapted by Irenaeus (2nd century), in *Upper Room Worshipbook* © 2006. Used by permission of Upper Room Books.

"Skills for Group Discernment," developed by John Anderson, adapted from Suzanne Farnham et al., "Discernment Listening Guidelines," in *Grounded in God: Listening Hearts Discernment for Group Deliberations.* Used by permission.

"Stages of Group Discernment," based on *Discerning God's Will Together: A Spiritual Practice for the Church* by Danny E. Morris and Charles M. Olsen © 1997. Used by permission of Upper Room Books.

Evaluation

Let us know what you think about *The Way of Discernment*! You may prefer to copy these pages rather than tearing them from the book. Use additional paper if needed. Here are three options for sharing your insights and perceptions: (1) Mail the completed evaluation form to the address on page 143; (2) Fax your evaluation to (615) 340-1783; or (3) Visit the discussion room at www.CompanionsInChrist.org.

Describe your group's experience with *The Way of Discernment*.

In what ways did the resource lead participants to a fuller understanding of spiritual formation and to a more experiential knowledge of spiritual practices?

What would improve *The Way of Discernment*?

Do you have follow-up plans for your group? If you have not already completed it, do you plan to begin the twenty-eight-week *Companions in Christ* foundational course or several of its parts?

What other kinds of resources are you looking for? What other topics would you like to see in the Companions in Christ series?

Mail to: Companions in Christ
c/o Editorial Director
Upper Room Ministries
P.O. Box 340004
Nashville, TN 37203-0004

About the Author

*M*arjorie J. Thompson has worked closely with all facets of *Companions in Christ* from its origins. Designing the foundational twenty-eight-week resource, writing articles and leader's guides for various titles in the Companions series, and training Companions trainers, she has helped guide and shape this small-group ministry for more than a decade.

Marjorie brings over twenty-five years of experience with retreat work, teaching, and writing in the area of Christian spiritual formation to her work as director of Pathways in Congregational Spirituality with Upper Room Ministries. She is the author of *Soul Feast: An Invitation to the Christian Spiritual Life* (Westminster/John Knox Press 1995/2005) and *Family, The Forming Center: A Vision of the Role of Family in Spiritual Formation* (Upper Room Books, 1996). An ordained minister in the Presbyterian Church (USA), she has served in pastoral ministry and as adjunct instructor in several seminary settings. Marjorie's educational path includes Swarthmore College, McCormick Theological Seminary, and a research fellowship at Yale Divinity School, where she was deeply influenced by her mentor, Henri J. M. Nouwen.